Expect More
Demanding Better Libraries For Today's Complex World

R. David Lankes

Expect More
Demanding Better Libraries For Today's Complex World
R. David Lankes

For more on the book, to join the conversation, or for volume discounts visit http://www.riland.org.

This book is dedicated to my wife Anna Maria. You have been patient as I have written, traveled, and struggled. You have been rightly impatient when I have ignored things that were much more important, like the boys, you, and enjoying life. Through all things you have shown the most amazing ability to tether me to reality and inspire me to reach for the stars.

Acknowledgements

Dean Liz Liddy and Syracuse University's School of Information Studies.

Cindy Hlywa for being the first reader of a very early draft.

Amy Behr for research and editing assistance.

Thanks to my editorial crew: Mia Breitkopf, copyeditor and fact-checker; Chelsea Neary, indexer; Loranne Nasir and Emma Montgomery draft editors.

Lauren Britton for working with my kids on the MakerBot.

Sue Considine and the Fayetteville Free Library for their inspiration and support. Sue, you run a hell of a shop!

The librarians of the Jamesville-Dewitt Central School District for their excellent service and research.

Beta Testers (early readers and reactors)
Victoria Williams
Dori Farah
Janice Dowling
Marcia Hayden-Horan
Nicolette Sosulski
Lauren Britton
Sue Considine
Kathryn Deiss
Elizabeth Stephens
William Schickling
Marguerite Avery
Sue Corieri

Table of Contents

Introduction

I believe that great librarianship, the kind you should expect, crosses boundaries. Great librarianship is great whether it is in academia, or the public sphere, or K–12 schools. For that reason, this book is not about expecting more from public libraries or from school libraries, but from all libraries. School libraries have a lot to teach all good libraries about issues of assessment and learning. Public libraries have a lot to share about working with a wide range of demographics. Academic libraries understand the power of knowledge creation. Corporate libraries, and the ever-present bottom line, can teach us all about measuring impact.

Throughout this book I will use the word communities a lot. I mean this term in a very broad sense. While I will talk more about this in Chapter 6, the bottom line is that a community is a set of people who come together around a commonality. Communities form where people live, and where they study or work. A university is a community, as is a law practice, as is a hospital.

My goal in this book is to show you the potential of libraries. That potential will never be realized if libraries or their communities build up rigid boundaries. You can use what works in little libraries to inform your big library. Ideas that start in public libraries can be successfully used in academia or businesses.

Where I can, I have tried to include examples from multiple types of libraries. However, realize that this is more about building bridges than erecting walls. You should expect your library and your community to look across all categories of libraries for what works, and not be so rigid about what they choose to consider "peer institutions." Innovation comes from everywhere and it is up to us to fit that innovation to our world.

A Special Note for Librarians

This book is for you to use when working with your communities. The main ideas are explored in much greater depth and in a more librarian-centric way in *The Atlas of New Librarianship*[1]. If you would like to promote or build on concepts you find here (or are looking for more reasons to disagree) I recommend reading the *Atlas*.

[1] Lankes, R. D. (2011). *The atlas of new librarianship*. Cambridge, Mass: MIT Press.

1. The Arab Spring: Expect the Exceptional

The Arab Spring had come to Egypt. In early 2011, on the heels of a successful revolution in Tunisia, Egyptians took to the streets to demand reforms from a government regime that had been in power for nearly 30 years. While much of the media fixated on protestors who occupied Tahrir Square in the Egyptian capital of Cairo, many protests started in the port city of Alexandria. In Alexandria, as in Cairo, people from across generations and the socio-economic scale rioted to demand liberty, justice, and social equity. In an attempt to restore the constitution, what was seen primarily as a peaceful uprising lead to the deaths of at least 846 people, and an additional 6,000 injured[2] across Egypt. On January 28 at 6 pm, after the prisons had opened, releasing murderers and rapists onto the street, all security withdrew from the streets of Alexandria. Roving gangs of looters took to the streets to take advantage of the chaos.

In Egypt's port city, the violence and looting devastated government buildings. Where offices once stood, only burned-out rubble remained.

---

[2] http://en.wikipedia.org/wiki/2011_Egyptian_revolution—Yes, a librarian and university professor just cited Wikipedia. I do it a lot throughout the book. There is nothing inherently wrong or non-credible in Wikipedia. In fact, it is more transparent in the construction of information than most published encyclopedias. I cite it because it is easy for the reader to get to, it is a great jumping-off point through references to other works, and I have verified the information in other sources…like we all should do.

Protestors went from building to building pulling down the symbols of corrupt power. Some looters and protestors then began to eye the Library of Alexandria.

President Mubarak, the focus of the uprising, had opened the modern library in 2002 at a cost of about $220 million. According to the library's website, Mubarak built it to "recapture the spirit of openness and scholarship of the original,"[3] the famous ancient Library of Alexandria—one of the wonders of the ancient world.

As it became apparent that the library might be in danger, protestors joined hands and surrounded the Library of Alexandria. Their goal was not to attack it or raid it, but to protect it. Throughout the protests and looting, the protestors—women, men and children—stood firm and protected the library. In essence, they were retaking the library for the people. After the uprising had subsided, when President Mubarak had stepped down and the protestors were celebrating their victory around the country, not a window of the library had been broken, not a rock thrown against its walls. Why, in the midst of tearing down the regime, did the people of the nation protect the library?

Why?

Why are stories like this, while maybe not quite so dramatic, repeated across the U.K. and the United States? As cities faced with a devastating financial crisis sought to close library branches, citizens rallied. Protestors disrupted town halls and city council meetings. Citizens picketed, and in Philadelphia, the City Council went so far as to sue the Mayor over the closing of libraries.

In Kenya, the government is building public libraries throughout the country, in rural and urban areas alike. Where the communities are too remote, they have built book carts—5,000 books in a wooden cart pulled by donkeys. In the even more remote northern sections of the country, they strap carts and tents to camels. Inside the villages, the carts are opened and the tents erected to allow parents and children an opportunity to learn. In these villages, camels provide transportation, labor, milk, and meat; even their dung is dried to power stoves. Now this essential animal is seen as providing another critical service: bringing knowledge to the people.

In the countryside along the coast of Colombia, Luis Soriano urges along his two donkeys, Alfa and Beto. On the backs of the donkeys are crates of books. Luis, a primary school teacher by trade, carries a sign reading "Biblioburro." He is bringing books to small villages and spreading literacy throughout the countryside to children who have seen too much violence and conflict for their years. He began with 70 books.

---

[3] http://www.bibalex.org/aboutus/overview_en.aspx (accessed May 19, 2012)

Through donations he has grown the collection to over 4,800 volumes, far past the capacity of his four-legged friends. He now houses the collection in a half-built room that has become an official satellite to the Santa Maria Community Library, some 180 miles away[4].

We find libraries in the finest castles of Europe and in the midst of the Occupy Wall Street populist protests in the States. Libraries are embraced by the elite and the commoner alike. We find librarianship in jungles and deserts, in schools, corporations, and in government agencies.

When we try to discover why, we find that there is power in libraries and steel in librarians. It goes deeper than tradition, buildings, and books. The reason for the protests and protectiveness over libraries is not found in collections of materials or columns and architecture. To find the answer to this riddle, one must look past the buildings and the books to the professionals who, throughout history, have served humanity's highest calling—to learn.

Libraries and librarians stood at the center of a growing Egyptian empire in the third century BC and the expansion of mathematics in Arabia in the fourteenth century.[5] Libraries helped bring Europe out of the Dark Ages and into the Renaissance, and helped democracy thrive in a post-colonial United States of America. Now, with the advent of the Internet and a new digital age, librarians are once again pointing the way towards a better society, founded in knowledge and giving respect to diverse views. This book is about what libraries and librarians can tell us about creating a brighter future and what kind of libraries and librarians we are going to need to make that future a reality.

Today's librarians are using the lessons learned over that nearly 3,000-year history to forge a new librarianship based not on books and artifacts but on knowledge and community. They are taking advantage of the technological leaps of today to empower our communities to improve. The librarians of today are radical positive change agents in our classrooms, boardrooms, and legislative chambers. They built the web before we called it the web. They were crowdsourcing knowledge and searching through mountains of information before Google, before Facebook, and even before indoor plumbing. Today's new librarians are not threatened or made obsolete by the Net. They are pushing the Net forward and shaping the world around you—often without your notice.

The field of librarianship represents an investment of nearly $7 billion in the U.S. and $31 billion worldwide.[6] In an age when traditional institutions are declining, library usage has grown steadily over the past

[4] see http://en.wikipedia.org/wiki/Biblioburro (accessed May 8, 2012), and
http://www.nytimes.com/2008/10/20/world/americas/20burro.html (accessed May 8, 2012)
[5] http://www-history.mcs.st-and.ac.uk/HistTopics/Arabic_mathematics.html (accessed May 8, 2012)
[6] http://www.oclc.org/us/en/reports/2003libsstackup.htm (accessed May 19, 2012)

twenty years. Did you know that there are more public libraries than McDonald's restaurants in the U.S. and that Americans go to libraries nearly three times more often than they go to the movies?[7] By understanding librarians and libraries we can understand how to build credibility and trust in a community overwhelmed with change and choices. We can discover how to create an environment to disagree and maintain a civil discourse. Ultimately, by understanding new librarianship, we can even understand something as grand as the role of a citizen in society.

Perhaps the biggest "why" question you can ask, and the one at the center of this book, is why do so many people see librarianship as antiquated, conservative, and less-than-inspiring? Why is it that while folks love the idea of libraries and librarians, they are quick to limit them to books or children, or simply think of them as historical holdovers? The answer is not that these people are wrong, but that they need to expect more. Too many libraries *are* about books. Too many librarians are reliving history and are stuck in a sort of professional conservatism that favors what they do over why they do it. Too many librarians see their collections, not the community, as their jobs. Too many libraries are seeking to survive instead of innovate, and promote the love of reading over the empowerment of the populations they serve. I am not claiming that these librarians are the majority, but they are too numerous and their communities (you) expect too little of them.

This book is written not for those librarians but for the people who either support or oversee libraries. This includes college provosts, students, parents, board members, volunteers, and, well, just about everyone who has ever gone to school or pays local taxes. You need to know what libraries are capable of, and you need to raise the bar on your expectations.

Throughout this book you are going to find examples of amazing libraries and librarians. Today, many in the field would call them exceptional, just as you might call the librarians in Egypt and Kenya exceptional. This is the root of the problem. These libraries may have been in exceptional circumstances, but their dedication to service and their connection to their communities should not be seen as exceptions to the norm. They should be the norm to which all libraries aspire.

In this book, you are going to read about a public library that has created a Fab Lab—a space where the community can work with 3D printers and make new inventions. You are going to read about a school library where the librarian is too busy helping teachers raise their performance to shelve books. You are going to read about librarians

---

[7] American Library Association (2010). Quotable facts about America's libraries. Retrieved from http://www.ala.org/ala/aboutala/offices/ola/quotablefacts/QF.3.8.2010.pdf

creating new companies in rural Illinois and transforming lives in Dallas. These are brilliant libraries and librarians, but if you see them as exceptional—as above and beyond the norm—you expect too little of your library.

Here is the key to a successful library: you. In a city or a Fortune 500 company, the library must shape itself around you and the goals of your community. If your community strives for greatness, the library should be great. If you are concerned about the future, or the economy, or the future of democratic discourse in this country, your library should be concerned as well. If you make these expectations known, if you arm yourself with what is possible and not what is, then the library and librarians can meet those expectations and goals. Of course, this is a two-way street. Great libraries expect a lot of their communities as well. Yes, great libraries require financial support, but even more than that they require open communication about your needs, your challenges, and your dreams.

This book will not be a love letter to libraries. I am not trying to turn you into a librarian. Instead, this is meant to begin an honest and realistic dialog about the place of libraries and librarians in your communities. Join me now as we explore the true potential of libraries and librarians.

2. The Argument for Better Libraries: Expect Impact

Cushing Academy is an elite prep school about 70 miles west of Boston. On its lush wooded campus, 445 students from 28 states and 28 countries work through high school. It is also, if you believe the Boston Globe[8], the end of libraries as we know them.

In 2009, Cushing invested hundreds of thousands of dollars renovating its library. A large part of that investment was getting rid of all physical books and replacing them with eReaders and digital resources. At least, that's what the Globe reported. The truth is more complex. Cushing did indeed get rid of a large number of printed books, mostly out-of-date research texts. It did this in order to actually expand the collection of materials available to students through digital means. It also increased the library staff and allowed students to access the resources of the library 24/7[9].

The interesting part of this story is not that a school eliminated its print collection (it didn't), or even the changing nature of the library's

---

8

http://www.boston.com/news/local/massachusetts/articles/2009/09/04/a_library_without_the_books/ (accessed May 8, 2012)

[9] http://roomfordebate.blogs.nytimes.com/2010/02/10/do-school-libraries-need-books/# (accessed May 8, 2012)

collection (increasingly digital). No, the interesting part of this story is the press reaction to the changes at a small boarding school. In headlines like "Digital School Library Leaves Book Stacks Behind," and "Welcome to the library. Say goodbye to the books.," reporters seemed to push past the nuance of a school expanding its library and looked for the end of libraries.

The central argument of this book is that we need better libraries. This presupposes that we need libraries in the first place. There are plenty of voices that question the need for any library. Before we jump into what you should expect from your library, it is worth reviewing the arguments for libraries in the first place.

The core arguments for libraries throughout time and today cluster around a few key themes:

- Collective Buying Agent
- Economic Stimulus
- Center of Learning
- Safety Net
- Steward of Cultural Heritage
- Cradle of Democracy
- Symbol of Community Aspirations

In truth, these cases for libraries are rarely made in isolation and many of them have fuzzy boundaries, but it is worth looking at them and showing how we must expect more of how these cases are made. Let's take these one at a time.

Collective Buying Agent

Stewart Brand famously said, "information wants to be free." At least, that is what everyone quotes him as saying. The full quote is:

> "On the one hand information wants to be expensive, because it's so valuable. The right information in the right place just changes your life. On the other hand, information wants to be free, because the cost of getting it out is getting lower and lower all the time. So you have these two fighting against each other."[10]

We see the results of this fight all over the place. Books and music are cheaper because distribution and production costs have been greatly diminished through digital networks. Academics are increasingly putting their papers online, and sites like YouTube show there is a healthy community willing to share video and content of all sorts for free. However, take a deeper look and you see that "free" isn't as cheap as it is

---

[10] http://en.wikipedia.org/wiki/Information_wants_to_be_free (accessed May 8, 2012)

cracked up to be. YouTube videos are free to watch—as long as you also watch a few commercials, just like broadcast TV.

Have you seen your cable bill recently? Not free? Movie ticket prices are rising and, if you want to get medical advice beyond WebMD, you better have health insurance. Business models are changing, but quality information or personalized information still costs real money.

To that end, libraries have always been one way in which communities pool resources to make big purchases. In universities, these purchases are things like academic journal subscriptions. In public libraries, pooled resources means shared popular reading material. In schools, it is article database subscriptions and media. In law offices, this includes LexisNexis and legal resource databases like Westlaw. The point is that if a resource is too expensive for one person and that resource has general utility, then pooling community assets (taxes, tuition, and departmental budgets) makes sense. In fact, when libraries find materials have become too expensive, they even team up into consortia.

To give you a small sense of how much money we are talking about, let me show you two quick examples. The first is a table put together by the University of Iowa that shows how much it costs for the University to provide academic journal titles electronically to faculty and staff:[11]

Publisher	Cost	# of Titles
Elsevier	$ 1,641,530	2095
Wiley/Blackwell	$ 868,031	1304
Springer	$ 607,540	400
Sage	$ 243,647	608
JSTOR	$ 97,602	2319
Cambridge UP	$ 43,940	145
Project Muse	$ 33,210	500
Oxford UP	$ 21,313	250

You read that right. It costs over $3.5 million a year for 7,621 journal titles. Oh, and by the way, that's per year. The library never owns those articles. We'll come back to that when talking about libraries as "of the community" in Chapter 5.

Of course, you may consider that cheap when you see what the state of Texas found. The state runs a service called TexShare through its State Library and Archive Commission (TSLAC). TexShare provides large databases of research information to the citizens of Texas through participating libraries.

---

[11] http://blog.lib.uiowa.edu/transitions/?p=720&utm_source=dlvr.it&utm_medium=twitter (accessed May 7, 2012)

Here's what Texas found in terms of cost:

"It would have cost the 677 libraries participating in the TexShare database program $97,044,031 dollars to purchase the database subscriptions that were purchased by the TSLAC for $7,042,558."[12]

$90 million in savings—that's the power of collective purchasing.

There are two factors that sometimes get lost when talking about libraries as collective buying agents: purchased items need organization, and using common funds should contribute to the common good. Let's start with items needing organization.

For my son's fifth birthday, my wife and I bought him 10 pounds of Legos from eBay. It turns out, when kids move out of the house and leave behind a drawer full of Legos, some parents box them up, weigh them, and sell them. This works great for a 5-year-old with an imagination, but not if he or she wants to build a particular thing. Lego is about imagination, but it is also about instructions and putting together sets around particular themes (space, Star Wars, etc.). Simply buying Legos by the pound doesn't serve this purpose. The situation is the same with books or databases in a library. You need to invest in people who can organize these purchased (or more often these days, licensed) materials. (We'll come back to this in Chapter 7 when we talk about librarians.)

The second concept that can get lost in the discussion of libraries as purchasing agents is the notion of the common good. That is, if a community (a school, a city, a college) pools its money to acquire things, those things should benefit the community as a whole. That may seem obvious, but libraries and communities can miss this point. Let's take a relatively new service called Freegal.[13]

Libraries subscribe to Freegal to allow library card holders to download music from the Sony music collection as MP3 files. Libraries purchase blocks of downloads (for example, 500 downloads for the community). This sounds like a great service, except that the library (and therefore the community) is paying to allow one library user to download a song for that member's personal use. If another library member wants that song, it will require another download. The libraries (read "the community") paying for the service cannot collect these songs and lend them out or archive them.

---

[12] https://www.tsl.state.tx.us/texshare/facts_ataglance.html (accessed May 8, 2012)

[13] http://www.freegalmusic.com/homes/aboutus (accessed May 8, 2012)—Yup that's it, that's the entire web presence for this company. Check out the Librarian in Black for a perspective on the service http://librarianinblack.net/librarianinblack/2011/04/just-say-no-to-freegal.html (accessed May 8, 2012)

Imagine walking into a library, asking for a book, and having the librarian go over to a bookstore to purchase it and then hand it to you to keep. Is this a wise use of community resources? Now imagine using tax funds to build a private road that only one citizen can use. It builds no common resource, brings no economy of scale, and ultimately uses the community pool to enrich individuals.

Freegal is an example of wealth redistribution at its worst. The mission of libraries is not about wealth redistribution. You must expect it to build a commons—a common infrastructure for the whole community to use.

Economic Stimulus

Related to the collective buying agent argument is the idea that libraries of all types boost the economy of the community.

In Indiana researchers found that:

"Libraries are a good value. The direct economic benefits that communities receive from libraries are significantly greater than the cost to operate the libraries."

Specifically:

- Indiana communities received $2.38 in direct economic benefits for each dollar of cost.
- Public library salaries and expenditures generate an additional $216 million in economic activity in Indiana.
- Academic library salaries and expenditures generate an additional $112 million in economic activity in Indiana.[14]

In Wisconsin they are apparently even better at getting value for their dollar, finding that:

"The total economic contribution of Wisconsin public libraries to the Wisconsin economy is $753,699,545. The return on investment in library services is $4.06 for each dollar of taxpayer investment."[15]

---

[14] Indiana State Library. (2007). The economic impact of libraries in Indiana. Retrieved from http://www.ibrc.indiana.edu/studies/EconomicImpactofLibraries_2007.pdf
[15] NorthStar Economics, Inc. (2008). The economic contribution of Wisconsin public libraries to the economy of Wisconsin. Retrieved from http://dpi.wi.gov/pld/pdf/wilibraryimpact.pdf

Just so you don't think I've cherry-picked two good states:

State	Return on $1 of Investment	Year of Study
Colorado	$5	2009[16]
Florida	$6.54	2004[17]
Wisconsin	$4.06	2008[18]
Indiana	$2.38	2007[19]
Pennsylvania	$5.50	2007[20]
South Carolina	$4.48	2005[21]
Vermont	$5.36	2006–2007[22]
Region	Return on $1 of Investment	Year of Study
Charlotte, NC	$3.15–$4.57	2008–2009[23]
Saint Louis, MO	$4	1999[24]
Southwestern Ohio	$3.81	2006[25]
Suffolk County NY	$3.93	2005[26]
Pittsburgh, PA	$3.05	2006[27]

[16] Steffen, N., Lietzau, Z., Curry Lance, K., Rybin, A. & Molliconi, C. (2009). Public Libraries—A wise investment: A return on investment study of Colorado libraries. Retrieved from http://www.lrs.org/documents/closer_look/roi.pdf

[17] Griffiths, J., King, D. W., Lynch, T. (2004). Taxpayer return on investment in Florida public libraries: Summary report. Retrieved from http://dlis.dos.state.fl.us/bld/roi/pdfs/ROISummaryReport.pdf

[18] NorthStar Economics, Inc. (2008). The economic contribution of Wisconsin public libraries to the economy of Wisconsin. Retrieved from http://dpi.wi.gov/pld/pdf/wilibraryimpact.pdf

[19] Indiana State Library. (2007). The economic impact of libraries in Indiana. Retrieved from http://www.ibrc.indiana.edu/studies/EconomicImpactofLibraries_2007.pdf

[20] Griffiths, J., King, D. W., Aerni, S. E. (2007). Taxpayer return-on-investment (ROI) in Pennsylvania public libraries. Retrieved from http://www.palibraries.org/associations/9291/files/FullReport.pdf

[21] The School of Library and Information Science, University of South Carolina. (2005). The economic impact of public libraries on South Carolina. Retrieved from http://www.libsci.sc.edu/SCEIS/exsummary.pdf

[22] State of Vermont Public Libraries. (2006-2007). The economic value of Vermont's public libraries. Retrieved from http://libraries.vermont.gov/sites/libraries/files/misc/plvalue06-07.pdf

[23] The University of North Carolina at Charlotte Urban Institute. A return on investment strategy of the Charlotte Mecklenburg Library. (2010). Retrieved from http://ui.uncc.edu/sites/default/files/pdf/Library_ROI_Study_2010_Final_FullReport.pdf

[24] Holt, G. E., Elliott, D. & Moore, A. (1999). Placing a value on public library services. Retrieved from http://www.slpl.lib.mo.us/libsrc/resresul.htm

[25] Levin, Driscoll & Fleeter. (2006). Value for money: Southwestern Ohio's return from investment in public libraries. Retrieved from http://9libraries.info/docs/EconomicBenefitsStudy.pdf

[26] Kamer, P. M. (2005). Placing an economic value on the services of public libraries in Suffolk County, New York. Retrieved from http://scls.suffolk.lib.ny.us/pdf/librarystudy.pdf

[27] Carnegie Mellon University Center for Economic Development. (2006). Carnegie Library of Pittsburgh: Community impact and benefits. Retrieved from http://www.clpgh.org/about/economicimpact/CLPCommunityImpactFinalReport.pdf

Where does all the economic boosting come from? Well, in part it is from the collective buying power of libraries that was previously discussed. If you don't have to buy a book or rent a movie because you can use library resources, that's a boost. In part, it comes from the fact that libraries are employers with employees who pay taxes (and contribute to the local economy). But this goes beyond saving money. For example, recent studies show libraries actually lead to more book buying.[28] In higher education, "libraries are an important consideration when students select a university or college, and, as a result, academic libraries can help institutional admissions boost enrollment.[29]"

The economic impact of libraries also comes from intangibles like creating a civic environment to attract businesses and workforce development. More recently, during the economic downturn of the past few years, libraries have taken on an important role in helping job seekers. In some libraries, this is simply providing out-of-work folks with access to computers and résumé workshops. In other libraries, however, we see what happens when communities and librarians expect more.

For example, let's take a look at Transform U.[30] This is a project of several public libraries in Illinois. These librarians recognized that when people are looking for a job, they are often looking for a bigger change in life. Maybe they would be better suited to going back to school. Maybe they need social services to help them feed their families. They definitely need to feel a sense of respect and self-worth. To meet these needs, the librarians created partnerships with local colleges, social service agencies, and economic development agencies. Now, when job seekers go to their local library, they have a whole support network that helps them identify their long terms goals and navigate sometimes confusing application sites at colleges and government agencies. They are provided with simple web tools for job seeking or creating businesses from scratch. These librarians went beyond the resources that they collected directly to meeting the needs of the community.

A small library in rural Eureka, Illinois, shows another way in which libraries can contribute to economic development—entrepreneurship. When a woman approached the Eureka Public Library about starting a catering business, something wonderful happened. The woman had seen that there was a need for more lunch spots in town. She was a trained commercial chef and had an idea to start a new restaurant, but didn't

---

[28] http://www.publishersweekly.com/pw/by-topic/industry-news/publishing-and-marketing/article/49316-survey-says-library-users-are-your-best-customers.html (accessed May 8, 2012)
[29] Oakleaf, M. for the Association of College and Research Libraries. (2010). The value of academic libraries: A comprehensive research review and report. Retrieved from http://www.ala.org/acrl/sites/ala.org.acrl/files/content/issues/value/val_summary.pdf
[30] http://www.transformuportal.org (accessed May 8, 2012)

know how to proceed. Rather than simply point her to some resources on starting a business, the library gave her a corner of its property where once a week (at first) the woman could set up a lunch spot. Over time it became a regular spot. "Chef Katie" was able to create a successful catering business and the whole town benefited.[31]

Eureka is not alone in helping community members find jobs and start businesses. The Dallas Public Library has cleared a significant portion of its fifth floor, replacing bookshelves with desks and white boards. They invite local entrepreneurs to set up shop within the library, rent free. Rather than pitching their ideas in their own homes, these entrepreneurs now use conference rooms.

This start-up spirit is not limited to public libraries. Syracuse University's School of Information Studies has a strong emphasis on start-ups, often forming undergraduate students from around the campus into idea- and business-generating teams. Librarians sit down with these teams to do competitive analysis and research the novelty of the ideas. In corporations around the country, corporate libraries are breaking patents, sizing up the competition, and providing ongoing training to lawyers, doctors, and computer manufacturers to help grow businesses.

Libraries as we know them already provide economic benefits to their communities. However, as we move forward we can expect more of them in this regard. We should expect libraries of all types to save communities money, and help spark whole new industries.

Center of Learning

This argument for libraries rests on the widely held belief that the best learning happens in the richest information environment. In academic institutions, this has translated into libraries that seek to comprehensively collect scholarly works and journals. In public libraries, this has meant collecting materials on a wide variety of subjects, not just popular fiction. It is the reason that school libraries exist.

Literacy, learning, and scholarship have always been associated with libraries. In fact, most directors of libraries in the Middle Ages were scholars who also maintained the collection. This trend continues today— the U.S. Library of Congress is headed by a historian.

In the 1900's, this argument—that libraries are places of learning— drove the work of public libraries as the "people's university." Melvil Dewey, father of the Dewey Decimal System, believed public libraries and public schools were "coequal" education institutions. In fact, public libraries did not collect fiction or any popular material because folks at the

---

[31] http://www.eurekapl.org (accessed May 8, 2012)

time did not connect general literacy, or "the love of reading" as we talk about it today, with learning.[32]

Today, libraries still have the concept of learning within their missions. One of the most successful national marketing campaigns in any industry is the American Library Association's "Read" posters that feature celebrities to encourage everyone to pick up a book and read. Summer reading programs encourage a habit of reading, a necessary skill for lifelong learning. School libraries are deeply engaged in literacy instruction, moving from basic reading skills, to research skills, to critical thinking exercises with the curriculum. Even academic and corporate libraries engage in literacy instruction, though focused on media and social literacy (like deciphering trends in social media, or understanding data visualizations).

However, while I assert that this argument for libraries is increasingly important, it is often a vague justification. For example, is it enough to create a resource-rich environment to facilitate learning? If I were to drop off a two-year-old in the middle of a well-stocked library, could I expect to come back in two days and have the child reading? Of course not.

Part of expecting more from your library and librarians is to force them to move past common-sense sounding arguments and into measurable activities. For example, does your public library work directly with K–12 school districts? How does an academic library's collection match the degree programs being offered at a college? What courses, curriculum, and services are being offered, by whom, to whom, and with what outcome? Simply stockpiling resources is not enhancing education. It is hoarding.

We will return to these themes throughout the rest of this book, but for now let us move on to libraries and the social safety net.

Safety Net

When you think of the social safety net, you probably think about the poor. To be sure, libraries provide access to a world of resources and services to those least able to afford it. However, the safety net that libraries extend goes far beyond one socioeconomic stratum. Very few individuals can afford the hundreds of thousands of dollars libraries pay for searchable databases. But the safety net argument goes beyond simply paying for resources, as well.

---

[32] Kruk, M. (1998). Death of the public library: From 'people's university' to 'public-sector leisure centre'. The Australian Library Journal. 47(2), 157. Retrieved from http://www.eric.ed.gov/ERICWebPortal/search/detailmini.jsp?_nfpb=true&_&ERICExtSearch_Se archValue_0=EJ572213&ERICExtSearch_SearchType_0=no&accno=EJ572213

Public libraries have long brought information to those otherwise unable to acquire it. This is in part the buying agent mission we talked about before, but today's safety net also includes bringing Internet access to rural America. These days, libraries are adding Internet connections to small village libraries and bookmobiles as a way of serving people in rural locations. A 2008 study showed that three-quarters of public libraries are the only provider of free access to the Internet in their community.[33] In Vermont, the state government is building a gigabit fiber optic network that will connect rural libraries across the state, making each library an access point for village businesses and homes.

In these days of digital networks, libraries of all types have extended the social safety net beyond access, to bridge the new growing digital divide—knowledge. While there is still a significant challenge in getting people connected to the Internet, and while digital tools are becoming increasingly necessary to life and work, the challenge is now helping people take advantage of these new tools. For example, after Christmas 2011, public libraries were flooded with people who had received iPads and Kindle Fires for the holiday. Many had bought or received the tablets unaware that you needed a wireless network to use them. So librarians helped set up the devices and showed folks how they could use the library's wireless network to get books, music, and video.

If you extend this idea of filling the knowledge gap you see that it is not just public libraries that are filling holes in safety nets. School libraries are now loaning out books not only to students, but to their parents as well. In every academic library, librarians are providing the students basic research skills that are not covered in classes. Law librarians are adding vital information literacy to the legal skills of lawyers and judges alike. In the U.S. Department of Justice, some librarians are now part of prosecutorial teams; their main job is researching expert witnesses to debunk their testimony in court.

Here we again come to a point where we must expect more of libraries as we move forward. As governments shrink in the face of economic austerity, they are withdrawing direct support to the public. Tax services, job services, and social services are all shrinking their footprint and expecting libraries to pick up the slack as public contact points. As résumés go online, as business with the government goes online, and as literature and music go online, we need libraries and librarians prepared to go beyond handing out forms and pointing to computers. We need

---

[33] American Library Association. Libraries connect communities: Public library funding & technology access study 2007-2008. (2008). Retrieved from
http://www.ala.org/research/sites/ala.org.research/files/content/initiatives/plftas/previousstudies/0708/LibrariesConnectCommunities.pdf

librarians to teach, solve problems, and ultimately advocate on behalf of the community.

Steward of Cultural Heritage

On the third floor of the Philadelphia Free Library's Central Library, you will find a library—yes, another library inside the Free Library. It is the library of William McIntyre Elkins, a rich investment banker of Philadelphia at the turn of the twentieth century and noted collector of books.[34] This is not a re-creation made to look like the original; it was moved in its entirety from Elkins' house to the Free Library. Not just the books, but the desk, the globe, the wood-paneled walls, the carpet—the whole library of Elkins. It is, frankly, a bit disconcerting to walk into. However, it is not unusual for larger libraries to have these special collections.

The importance of libraries to the preservation of our cultural heritage is not an argument you hear that often these days. The emphasis over the past 30 years has been on information and resources that have direct and immediate impact on scholarship, learning, and recreation. However, over the centuries and in many other countries, the preservation of the cultural record (art work, manuscripts, and such) was the primary reason behind libraries. It's why you will find an original folio of Shakespeare's works in the Dallas Public Library, and a Gutenberg Bible at the University of Texas' Ransom Center.

In the Nordic countries, libraries are often collocated with museums and theaters. And, to this day, if you go to Italy and look for a public library, you will be hard pressed to find one. That is because they are not there for the casual user; they are there for the scholar or the student. As one Italian librarian put it to me, "In Italy we don't ask the library for a recipe for sauce; we ask our mothers." In other words, the library is not for daily tasks.

Many U.S. libraries, particularly academic libraries, still build amazing collections of art and historical treasures. But the language of cultural heritage in libraries is also changing. Today, in addition to preserving cultural artifacts of the past, librarians are working with neighborhoods to capture the culture of the now. Ken Lavender, a professor of practice at Syracuse University, works with volunteers and students to go into the neighborhoods of Syracuse. There they work with residents to capture stories, digitize shoeboxes full of photos, and create oral histories so the residents can pass their heritage down to future generations.

---

[34] Shaffer, E. (1956). *Portrait of a Philadelphia collector: William McIntire Elkins (1882*–1947). Retrieved from http://libwww.freelibrary.org/dickens/Elkins_Portrait_Essay.pdf

Our history and how we saw ourselves in the past are vital parts of how we move forward. However, we should now expect our libraries to not simply act as a storehouse of the works of great men of the past, but to also capture our story as it is unfolding today. Take the Elkins Library in Philadelphia. If you want to see it, you take an elevator to the third floor and ring a buzzer. Within about 20 minutes someone will let you in to see it. We need our history at our fingertips so we can weave it into our future.

Cradle of Democracy

To be clear, you can have libraries without democracy and democracy without libraries—one need only look through history. However, I would argue that in order to have a true liberal democracy, libraries are a requirement.

The United States is a liberal democracy. Canada is a liberal democracy. France, Germany, India, and Israel are liberal democracies, too. The "liberal" part of liberal democracy has nothing to do with a political party, or even how socially progressive a country is; it refers to the belief that democracy is more than voting. A liberal democracy also includes protections of civil liberties and a constitutional protection from intrusive governmental power. It is an important modifier. Iraq, under Saddam Hussein, was nominally a democracy. Hussein was elected president with 99% of the vote. However, few would consider this a truly liberal democracy.

Why are libraries so important for a liberal democracy? The short answer is that a true democracy requires the participation of an informed citizenry. The core mission of libraries, public and otherwise, is creating a nation of informed and active citizens.

When library supporters make this argument, they will often use one or more of these three quotes:

"The people are the only censors of their governors; and even their errors will tend to keep these to the true principles of their institution.... The way to prevent these [errors] is to give them full information of their affairs through the channel of the public papers, and to contrive that those papers should penetrate the whole mass of the people. The basis of our governments being the opinion of the people, the very first object should be to keep that right; and were it left to me to decide whether we should have a government without newspapers, or newspapers without a government, I should not hesitate a moment to prefer the latter. But I should mean that every man should receive those papers, and be capable of reading them." – Thomas Jefferson

"There is not such a cradle of democracy upon the earth as the Free Public Library, this republic of letters, where neither rank, office, nor wealth receives the slightest consideration." – Andrew Carnegie

"A popular government without popular information, or the means of acquiring it, is but a Prologue to a Farce or a Tragedy; or perhaps both. Knowledge will forever govern ignorance; and a people who mean to be their own Governors must arm themselves with the power which knowledge gives." – James Madison

All three of these quotes share a common message: an informed citizen is necessary to sustain a democracy. However, each of these quotes emphasizes a different facet of maintaining and participating in a democracy. Jefferson is talking about transparency, Carnegie access, and Madison education. Good libraries take on all three of these. Let's start with transparency.

Democracy and Transparency

In the preceding quote, Jefferson is clearly talking about newspapers and the press, not libraries. Yet he is also emphasizing the necessity of transparency, which is a goal that librarians and journalists share. A functioning representative government of the people is not a "fire and forget" thing. You don't simply vote politicians into office and wait for the next election. There must be oversight of the actions of elected officials to prevent abuse and to shape civic discourse and policy. Watergate was not resolved through an election, but through the emergence of documents and evidence of corrupt actions on the part of the elected government.

Libraries further the goal of transparency in a number of ways. They work from within the government to document, archive, and disseminate the work of agencies. For example, if you want to know every law passed by the U.S. Congress, you can go to the Library of Congress' website and search the THOMAS Database.[35] If you would like access to research funded by the National Institutes of Health, click over to the National Library of Medicine and search the PubMed database.[36]

Libraries also further transparency outside of the federal government. Nearly 1,250 academic and public libraries around the country house government documents as part of the Federal Depository Library Program. If a government agency prints a report, brochure, form, or regulation, it is deposited at these libraries, which must ensure public access to these materials.

---

[35] http://thomas.loc.gov/home/thomas.php (accessed May 8, 2012)
[36] http://www.ncbi.nlm.nih.gov/pubmed (accessed May 8, 2012)

Beyond the federal level, every state has a publicly accessible law library that houses the laws, regulations, and judicial decisions of that state. Many local libraries store the proceedings of town councils and county legislatures. The idea is that citizens can observe the work of their governments and participate in decision making.

There are enormous challenges that libraries and all citizens face in terms of transparency (like archiving documents on ever-shifting websites, classification of documents, and more), but we'll return to those later.

Democracy and Access

What Carnegie talks about in the previous quote is equal access to the work of the state. Of course, he did more than just talk about it; he is considered a sort of patron saint of libraries after he built over 2,500 of them around the world[37].

In Carnegie's day, access meant access to the printed record of thoughts—books. Today, libraries of all sorts have extended that idea into many other channels. This is most clearly seen in the provision of the Internet and public access computers in the public libraries. However, it is also seen in policies of all libraries that give out library cards to all citizens in a community, free of charge. In many other countries you must pay a fee for a card or to use the computers. For example, in the Netherlands a library card costs 15 Euros per year or 30 Euros if you want to borrow books. If you would like to reserve books to borrow? 50 Euros.[38]

The importance of access is also seen in academic libraries that allow for public access instead of restricting access to the faculty and students of a given college or university. The importance of access is seen in the millions of dollars state libraries are spending on statewide database licenses, giving equal access to these resources to urban, suburban, and rural communities alike.

Of course, all the access in the world is useless if you don't know what to do with the information you are accessing. That was Madison's point.

Democracy and Education

Madison said, "A people who mean to be their own Governors must arm themselves with the power which knowledge gives." What I absolutely love about this quote is the use of the active verb "arm." Simply having access to the information generated by a working democracy is not enough. Being able to look up a law online is useless if

---

[37] http://carnegie.org/about-us/foundation-history (accessed May 8, 2012)
[38] http://www.oba.nl/index.cfm/t/Memberships/vid/8ECCC66F-0FD8-C5E6-AF193D1A891D3042 (accessed May 8, 2012)

you can't read. Of course, even if you can read, can we also assume you know how to actually use a computer and get online in the first place?

A functioning democracy must actively develop (or in Madison's words "arm") an educated population. This argument is central to the idea of public education in this country. Yet the public education sector is struggling with an increasingly codified curriculum and an 8% high school drop-out rate (17.6% in the Latino community).[39] The public elementary and secondary education system doesn't even touch the roughly 12% of the adult U.S. population who lack basic literacy skills.[40]

Public libraries, school libraries, and academic libraries are all a part of educating the citizenry for democratic participation. It is an expansion of the safety net argument, but rather than a safety net for economic participation or well-being, it is the safety net for how we govern ourselves.

Democracy and Higher Expectations

Democracy is not an easy thing. Democracy is not a neat and tidy. In our daily lives, few of us take the time from our commutes, e-mail, and daily struggles to think about where we fit in the democratic scheme of things. What's more is that in your library you can find the books and the computers, but where is the democracy? Is there an active effort by your library to prepare you to be an active citizen?

Let me be clear, this is not about being political and ideological. The point is not asking whether your library is lined up with a party or a candidate. Rather, it is asking what difference the library has made in the governance of your community (be it a town, a university, a school, or a corporation). Did you know that half of the Library of Congress' budget is devoted to something called the Congressional Research Service? The Congressional Research Service (CRS):

> *...works exclusively for the United States Congress, providing policy and legal analysis to committees and Members of both the House and Senate, regardless of party affiliation. As a legislative branch agency within the Library of Congress, CRS has been a valued and respected resource on Capitol Hill for nearly a century.*[41]

Does your library have a similar service to inform your local politicians, chancellor, president, CEO, or principal? Shouldn't having a good school library mean that you have a well-informed principal? Part of raising expectations for our libraries is to move past rhetorical loose connections between democracy, informed community, and libraries, or

---

[39] http://nces.ed.gov/fastfacts/display.asp?id=16 (accessed May 8, 2012)
[40] http://www.livescience.com/3211-14-percent-adults-read.html (accessed May 8, 2012)
[41] http://www.loc.gov/crsinfo (accessed May 8, 2012)

else risk making one of the most important arguments for libraries ring hollow.

Symbol of Community Aspirations

Libraries have always been about the ideas, aspirations, and dreams of the individual. Librarians can tell you amazing stories of people they have helped. From saving a woman from an abusive relationship, to lifting a homeless man from poverty, to saving the life of a cancer patient, to inspiring wonder in a child, libraries have had an impact on people's lives.

Frankly, what I wish librarians would talk more about are the hopes and aspirations of communities. Communities have dreams. They long to be world-class scholarly institutions or economic hubs. Communities dream about living comfortably or being market leaders. Sure, these dreams aren't as well-defined as those of individual community members, but they represent a sort of holistic desire that sets policy, assigns resources, and changes messages to the outside world.

Libraries have become aspirational institutions. At the most basic, the building itself serves as a symbol for the community and the community's desire to be associated with knowledge. San Francisco, Seattle, Salt Lake City, and Vancouver all used new library buildings to revitalize their downtowns. The inspiring architecture of libraries has become the new cathedral—a concrete way for a community to make a statement of its importance.

The power of architecture, and the statements we seek to make with library buildings in particular, cannot be denied. Donors at universities are naming libraries, and architects take great pride in academic libraries, sometimes celebrating the building over the library function itself.

When it comes to expecting more, however, we must look at the power of a building versus the power of the services housed within (and, more and more, outside). Barbara Quint, a reporter at Information Today's *Searcher* magazine, once said that a library after hours is like a coral reef without the fish—it is beautiful and serene but devoid of life. It is a remnant that can only remind us of a point in time.

Likewise, if you take away the librarians and the staff, but leave the books, the computers, and the architecture, you will have a fine sculpture of a library that will become a snapshot of the community's past. But, if you threw out the books and the buildings and left a dedicated group of library professionals, you could invite the public in and they would construct the future.

Now more than ever, the future of any community is not in the riches we pull from the ground or the glass we send streaming into the sky, but in the decisions and talents of the community members. They are not passive consumers of libraries or content, or an audience to democracy, but the very reason we are all here. They deserve a new librarianship, a new library that enables radical positive change. The reasons I have just covered support why we have libraries in general. Frankly, you will hear these arguments from good and bad libraries alike. The real question is how these themes and justifications become reality in your community and how they must transform for libraries to continue to be relevant in the future.

3. The Mission of Libraries: Expect More Than Books

The Syracuse University Library was full. There was no room left on the shelves. This is not an uncommon problem with libraries of all sorts, and the solutions range from throwing things away (weeding) to constructing new buildings. Syracuse tried the first, then the second, but finally settled on off-site storage. The librarians were going to take the least used items (those not checked out in about 10 years or so) and ship them to a warehouse five hours away. If an item from the warehouse was needed, it would be shipped back to Syracuse or digitized and sent directly to the computer of the professor or student who requested it.

You might think that there wouldn't be that many books going unused over a decade span, but you would be wrong. In fact if you pick just about any library you will run into something called the 80/20 rule. Of a collection, 80% of use will be from 20% of that collection. Put another way, you could throw away 80% of the books and still meet 80% of the requests from the community. So, why keep the rest? Well, you never know if one of those 20% of users will use one of those 80% of low-use books to cure cancer—and there is no way to know ahead of time.

The library at Syracuse University, though, was not throwing away the low-use books. It was just moving them. It seemed logical. However, the humanities departments on campus nearly rioted. Religion professors, history graduate students, English majors all went ballistic. They disrupted faculty senate meetings, staged protests in the library, and wrote rather pointed editorials. "Why can't we move the books to someplace local?" "This was a bad collection to begin with, now you're going to make it worse?"

While the librarians were expecting some resistance to the off-site plan, the level of pushback took them by surprise. For years, the librarians had been increasing use of the library. Through the introduction of a learning commons, lots of meeting spaces, a cafe, power strips, and new services, the library was being used more than ever. The library was full not only in terms of books, but in terms of people. The problem was, the humanities scholars didn't see the coffee and undergraduates plugged into power strips as an appropriate use of the space. Every table was a place for more shelves and more books. That, they said, was the purpose of the library—holding books and materials, not meeting spaces and coffee.

This idea, that libraries are about books, is hardly limited to humanities faculty. A few years earlier in Syracuse (apparently a hot spot for library controversy) the county started a book recycling program. Once a year residents could box up their old books and drop them off to be pulped. There were immediate cries from concerned citizens calling upon the public library to intervene. Don't recycle the books, donate them to the library! The library said no, not because it was full, but because it was too busy.

The library didn't have the staff to sort through the hundreds and hundreds of books looking for the right ones to keep—at least that is what they said initially. When community members started to organize the Boy Scouts to sort through the books, the real reason came to light. It turns out the librarians had already gone to the book recycling collection point and found old and rotting books of little value. They also found that residents took this as an opportunity to recycle items like *Hustler* magazine. The librarians weren't that interested in sorting through these shoulder to shoulder with Boy Scouts.

School libraries regularly receive donations of *National Geographic* because they "must" be valuable. Never mind that there is no place to store the physical magazines and the entire run of the magazine is available digitally.

In Glendale, an affluent suburban village outside of Cincinnati, the citizens started their own library with donated books. They lined the shelves and opened the doors. After the first week, traffic evaporated. It seems folks weren't looking to read the books that they had donated and were willing to drive to the three other public libraries within a five-mile radius.

All of these stories highlight one of the biggest myths about modern libraries—libraries are just about books. You can be forgiven if this is what you thought, too. After all, libraries have been very successful in the book business, and, moreover, many libraries have been building this book-library brand in their communities over the past century or so.

At first glance even the most famous library standards scream books. In 1931, S. R. Ranganathan proposed his five laws of librarianship[42]. These laws have become a cornerstone of library thought:

1. Books are for use.
2. Every reader his book.
3. Every book its reader.
4. Save the time of the reader.
5. The library is a growing organism.

Clearly, the idea that libraries are about books is deep in the DNA of librarianship.

However, let's look again. How central are books to those laws? Had Ranganathan lived 2,000 years ago, would he have said "scrolls are for use"? If you replace books with eBooks or web pages, do these ideas still hold true? I think they do. These laws really state that the center of the library is the community. The job of the library is to fulfill the needs of the community members, not simply to house materials.

Libraries, good ones and bad ones, have existed for millennia. Over that time, they have been storehouses of materials, certainly, but also places of scholarship, record keepers for nation states, and early economic development incubators. In fact, the idea that a library is a building filled to the rafters with books and documents is only about an 80-year-old view.

---

[42] http://babel.hathitrust.org/cgi/pt?id=uc1.b99721;page=root;view=image;size=100;seq=11

Take a look at the Free Library of Philadelphia today:

Figure 2: Present day music room at the Philadelphia Free Library

Books on shelves around the columns—a library. Now, take a look at the same part of the library from the late 1920's:

Figure 3: Music room of the Free Library of Philadelphia about 1927[43]

[43] Music Room of the Free Library of Philadelphia, circa 1927. 43Retrieved from
http://libwww.freelibrary.org/75th/SearchItem.cfm?ItemID=75A0262

Yes, that is the same department. Working tables, natural light—a space more for people and learning than for books.

When did we start thinking of libraries as book havens? Libraries have always housed collections of materials, but even this concept of repository is a relatively modern one. It was formed when libraries were seeking to create comprehensive collections at the same time as a dramatic drop in prices of paper and printing. It was only in the twentieth century that mass-produced books starting filling up libraries as well as living rooms and schools.

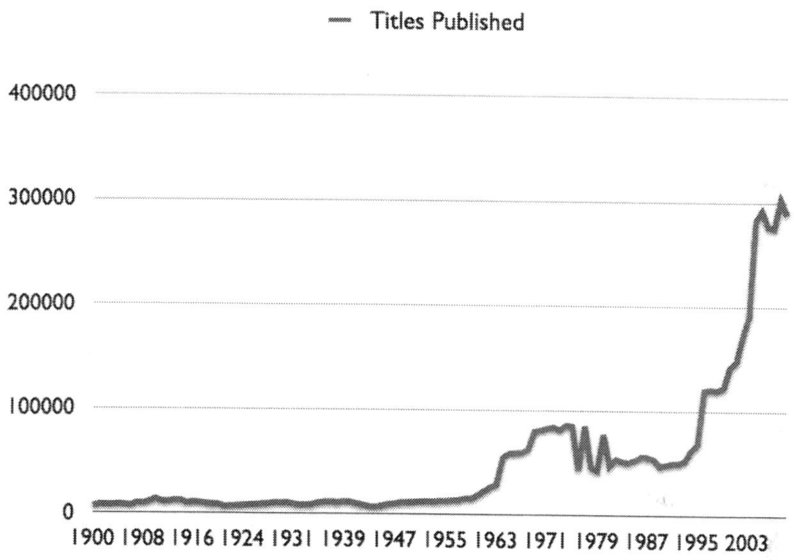

— Titles Published

Figure 4: Growth of titles published worldwide[44]

This bibliophilia changed how we look not only at libraries today, but libraries across history.

Let's take a look at the Library of Alexandria mentioned in the first chapter. The original library was a wonder of the world. Today, those who know of it think of it as an enormous collection of documents from the ancient world—and it was. My favorite story is about ships that would pull into the port of Alexandria, one of the busiest ports in the world at the time. Soldiers would meet the ships and confiscate any documents

[44] This data was compiled from the following sources:
Unesco. (1964). *Statistical yearbook: Annuaire statistique = Anuario estadístico*. Paris: Unesco.
Wright, W. E., R.R. Bowker Company & Council of National Library Associations. (1956). *American library annual for....* New York: R.R. Bowker.
The World almanac and encyclopedia. New York : Press Pub. Co. (The New York World)

they had on board (including those used as ballast). The documents would be taken to the library, copied, and the copies were returned to the ships.

But if you are thinking of the ancient library as a huge document storehouse, like the current picture of the Free Library of Philadelphia, you would be wrong. In fact, the Library of Alexandria was much more akin to the universities of today. There were multiple buildings on the campus. One of the first was a temple dedicated to the Muses called the Musae—where we get the word for museum. The main building of the Library was as much a dormitory as it was a warehouse. Scholars from the known world were brought together and encouraged to talk and create. It was, in fact, one of the earliest think tanks and innovation centers in history. The librarian was one of the closest advisors to the rulers of the city-state.

When the Library of Alexandria was destroyed, much of the collection eventually found a new home in Moorish Spain. There, these documents did not sit around but were translated, augmented, and used. This became apparent during the first crusades at the end of the medieval times. As crusaders "liberated" the city of Toledo, they found library after library after library. It must have been stunning to see that one of the 80 libraries held more volumes than did the entirety of France. More remarkable was that the citizens weren't simply preserving manuscripts, they were using them to develop new forms of architecture, new aqueducts, new modes of governance, and a little thing called algebra (including the whole concept of zero, by the way). In fact, one historian credits the living libraries of the Muslim world with the creation of universities and the Renaissance.

In Victorian England, public libraries had gaming parlors. Andrew Carnegie built over 2,509 libraries[45] around the world to encourage democratic participation and social opportunity. Public libraries have been art galleries. They have added children's collections when the modern concept of childhood was virtually created with the advent of child labor laws. They've even strapped a diesel engine onto the front of collections in the form of bookmobiles to serve rural and remote populations. My point is that if you think of a library as a bunch of books in a building (or worse, if your librarian thinks of it that way), you need to expect more—a whole lot more.

Today's great libraries are transforming from quiet buildings with a loud room or two to loud buildings with a quiet room. They are shifting from the domain of the librarians to the domain of the communities. What is guiding this transformation? What is shaping Ranganathan's "growing organism"? A long-held mission:

---

[45] http://carnegie.org/about-us/foundation-history (accessed May 8, 2012)

The mission of a library is to improve society through facilitating knowledge creation in the community.

To be clear, this is my wording, but the underlying concepts can be seen historically where scholars used to run libraries to advance the research agenda of their colleges. It can also be seen in the librarians of Kenya and Columbia who started off this book. Bad libraries only build collections. Good libraries build services (and a collection is only one of many). Great libraries build communities.

Stone tablets became scrolls, scrolls became manuscripts, manuscripts became books, and books are rapidly becoming apps. The tools that libraries use to achieve the mission, any mission, will change. The purpose of using those tools (and new tools) remains steady over long periods of time. Libraries should be about knowledge, not tools.

The rest of this book will take a look at what you need to expect out of a library based on components of the above mission statement (what do I mean by improve, by knowledge, by facilitate, etc.?), but before we do that we need to tackle two issues: reading and the general utility of a mission.

I Love Reading…No Really

Take a look at the mission again: improving society through facilitating knowledge creation. What ever happened to promoting a love of reading and/or books? Does expecting more from libraries mean abandoning reading and literature, fiction and poetry? The reason reading isn't in this larger mission is that not all libraries are centrally focused on reading. School libraries and public libraries see the promotion and expansion of reading skills as one of their core goals; corporate and academic libraries assume the people they serve already have these skills. What's more, while reading is a crucial skill to creating knowledge, it is not the exclusive route to "enlightenment." Some learn through reading, some through video, others through doing, and the vast majority through combining these. We should expect our libraries to support all of these modalities of learning.

When folks ask me about libraries, reading, and my proposed mission they are normally asking "can't I just use the library to read a good novel or borrow a DVD without worrying about saving the world? Isn't there value in just reading for recreation?" My answer is yes and that fiction is as important to learning and building knowledge as is non-fiction. Stories are how we dream and how we test our ethical bounds. A good novel can reveal fundamental truth in ways no academic tome of philosophy ever can. What's more, the ideas and inspirations for great action often come when we least expect it.

Much of library literature focuses on concepts of information and empowerment, often ignoring or silently assuming that libraries can still support recreation and reading development. To be sure, this book is focused on libraries as places of social engagement and learning. The question isn't "should libraries support recreational reading?" The answer to that question is dependent on the community—like supporting the arts or parks. The real question revolves around individuals who want to turn recreational reading into something social, or geared towards some larger goal.

So I read a book and love it. That may be enough for me. But what if a beautiful piece of fiction inspires me to write my own novel, or invent some new device, or form a group of others who love the book and seek to act. It is not the role of the library to predetermine the outcomes of reading (or inventing, or movie making)—that edges too close to telling people what to read and why. Rather, it is the place of the library to be a platform for the community members to turn their love and passion into something for the good of the community and/or themselves.

The more we do of something the better we get. So we need to support reading of all kinds where appropriate (in the library, in school, on the playground, on vacation, in the laboratory, in video games). When you read the words "knowledge" and "learning" throughout this book, don't think I am limiting that to just to the ideas that end up in textbooks and research articles. Poetry, novels, and a good science fiction story all carry equal weight to me in knowledge creation. However, I believe that we should also expect libraries of all kinds to be ready to support the outcomes of that reading.

So let us now turn our attention to how libraries tackle these ideas in their mission statements.

Mission to Nowhere?

A mission statement is an important thing. It represents a sort of consensus on what an organization thinks is important. It is in the mission that we can begin to see how libraries are setting expectations for themselves and the communities they serve. Let's take a look at statements from some libraries and organizations:

Let's start with a great mission from the New York Public Library:

"The mission of The New York Public Library is to inspire lifelong learning, advance knowledge, and strengthen our communities."[46]

You can't get much better than advancing knowledge and strengthening communities.

Speaking of advancing knowledge, check out the mission of the libraries of the Massachusetts's Institute of Technology:

"The mission of the MIT libraries is to create and sustain an intuitive, trusted information environment that enables learning and the advancement of knowledge at MIT. We are committed to developing innovative services, strategies, and systems that promote discovery, preserve knowledge, and improve worldwide scholarly communication. We empower MIT through knowledge."[47]

Now check out the Library of Congress':

"The Library's mission is to support the Congress in fulfilling its constitutional duties and to further the progress of knowledge and creativity for the benefit of the American people."[48]

Note that it is clear in defining its community: the American people, but only after the Congress.

For the parents, teachers, administrators, and those interested in schools, here are great mission statements from school libraries:

"The mission of Tehiyah Day School is to inspire curiosity, a strong sense of community, and a vibrant connection to Judaism. At Tehiyah, we live the curriculum!"[49]

and

"The mission of the school library media program is :
• to be an integral part of Whittier Elementary School and its surrounding community
• to provide collaboration with staff to create authentic learning for all students
• to provide quality resources and instruction to students and staff
• to encourage staff and students in becoming effective users of ideas and information

---

[46] http://www.nypl.org/help/about-nypl/mission (accessed May 8, 2012)
[47] http://libraries.mit.edu/about/mission.html (accessed May 8, 2012)
[48] http://www.loc.gov/about/mission.html (accessed May 8, 2012)
[49] http://www.tehiyah.org/Learning_at_Tehiyah/Library/mission.html (accessed May 8, 2012)

• to promote life-long reading and learning both for pleasure and for information"[50]

and

"The mission of the Howard County Public School System is to ensure excellence in teaching and learning so that each student will participate responsibly in a diverse and changing world."[51]

I love them—love them all. They show you that, across a range of institutions, the mission can be short and meaningful. They can also be about the impact the libraries want to have, not the stuff they collect. It is no accident that these organizations have international reputations.

With that in mind, let me turn to some not-so-inspiring missions. I have changed the names of all of the libraries to "MyTown" or "MyCollege" to protect the not so innocent.

The MyTown Public Library provides materials in a variety of formats and services for persons of all ages, to help community residents obtain information that meets their personal, educational, and professional needs. All library services are vigorously promoted to increase public awareness and thereby increase the quality of life for MyTown citizens.

Aside from the fact that this mission is clearly about the stuff the library collects, one feature of this mission drives me nuts. It is the mission of the library to promote the library? And not just to promote itself, but do so vigorously?! Isn't it a bit arrogant to say that simply by knowing the library is there, life will improve for citizens? Also, what should you expect from this library? Stuff, yes, but also a sort of "me first" attitude.

OK, next one:

The mission of the MyTown Public library shall be to:
Provide for the recreational needs of its patrons by supporting leisure time activities through the provision of library materials and services.
Provide for the collective and individual information needs of its patrons by selecting, acquiring, cataloging, organizing, and distributing information and materials.
Provide for the cultural enhancement of individual patrons and the MyTown community by providing materials and attendant activities that foster understanding of the development of international, national, community, and individual heritage and lifestyle.

---

[50] http://schools.fcps.org/whes/lmc/missionstatement.htm (accessed May 8, 2012)
[51] http://www.pingry.org/page.cfm?p=466 (accessed May 8, 2012)

Provide for the continuing educational needs of its patrons by supporting learning beyond that required for attaining academic degrees or meeting job qualifications by providing materials that enhance daily life, personal interests, and job performance.

The MyTown Library recognizes the impact of technology, specifically electronic communication and information, upon the MyTown community. The Library strives to identify, to retrieve, to organize, and to provide access to technology in its various formats. In fulfilling its mission, the MyTown Library fully supports the principle of freedom of expression and the public's right to know. The Library will foster an atmosphere of free inquiry and provide information without bias or discrimination.

Wow! Can you see printing that on a T-shirt? My main complaint here is that it is all about pushing out materials, not co-owning or creating them with the community. This is not about the library as a service, but instead about the library as a servant. It shows another interesting aspect of old versus new librarianship's worldview, namely the relationship of the library to the community.

Libraries *"for the people"* is an old way of looking at libraries. It sees the library as apart from the community, a service the community can use and pay for, but ultimately ignore or discard. The new view is the library "of the people." The community is an integral part of what the library does, and librarians are full-fledged members of the community. Librarians do their jobs not because they are servants or because they are building a product to be consumed by the community, but ultimately to make the community better. Community members don't support the library because they are satisfied customers, but because the library is part of who they are.

This concept of a library is analogous to democratic government. When the people feel part of the government, their views are represented, their voices are heard, and they are governing themselves (of the people). When, however, they feel the government is a sort of distant standing political class, dissatisfaction occurs (or, in the very extreme, you get the Arab Spring). Libraries must be of the people, not for them. When a member of the community walks into a library (or clicks into it), he or she must see an opportunity to contribute, to have a voice, and to improve the institution. Otherwise, the library is just another Borders or Blockbuster.

Likewise, the librarian seeks to provide excellent service not only out of an altruistic drive but out of a selfish desire to improve his or her own condition. If the librarian does his or her job well, the community will improve, and an improved community then improves the situation of the librarian. It is a virtuous circle.

Let's take a look at some discouraging academic library missions:

The University Library strengthens the MyCollege academic enterprise by providing, presenting, and preserving a wide range of information resources. We utilize innovative approaches in working with faculty and students to help them discover, use, manage, and share the array of information that supports their research, teaching, and learning.

To be honest, this one isn't too egregious, but it is still very much about strengthening an institution by providing stuff (information resources). Also, while innovation is good, it only extends to library functions in this case. It is not about helping innovators or fostering innovation within the community. It is also very much saying that faculty and students will improve by working with the library, but not about the library learning from (and preferably with) the community.

Next:

The mission of the MyCollege Library is to support the research and curricular needs of its faculty and students by providing a superb collection of legal materials and by offering the highest possible level of service. To the extent consistent with its mission, the Library supports the research needs of the greater MyCollege community as well as scholars from outside the MyCollege community requiring access to its unique collections.

In other words, come get your stuff here, and it is really great stuff. Let's move back to the public library for one more example:

The MyTown Library, a public service agency, is to provide all residents of the MyTown with a comprehensive collection of materials in a variety of media that records man's knowledge, ideas and culture, to organize these materials for ready access, and to offer guidance and encouragement in their use. Special emphasis is placed on popular materials in all formats to all ages and on providing a lifelong learning and education center for all residents of the community. The Library especially serves as a place for children to discover the joy of reading and the value of Libraries.

Where to start in this sort of kitchen sink, stuff-based example? How about doubting that this library has a comprehensive collection of man's knowledge, ideas, and culture? Talk about overpromising and under-delivering. Add to that serving everyone, and do we really want anyone indoctrinating children?

A Mission Based on Higher Expectations

So libraries are on a mission: to improve society through knowledge creation. Of course, the mission of libraries is unique among most other institutions. The mission of the library almost always sits within the mission of a larger organization. A public library is part of a city or county. An academic library is part of a college or university. School libraries are there to propel the overall mission of a school. Corporate libraries are there to contribute to the bottom line.

We will return to how the mission of improving society is ultimately shaped and shapes a community when I discuss what exactly I mean by "improve society" in Chapter 5. For now, let us turn to the more immediate concern of how libraries actually fulfill their mission. That is, first and foremost, what does a library do? To know this is especially important since a library does much more than simply collect books.

4. Facilitating Knowledge Creation: Expect to Create

It was an unusually warm winter in Syracuse. Still, it was quite cold as I made my way with my two boys, Riley (age 11) and Andrew (age 8), to the Fayetteville Free Library. Fayetteville is an affluent suburb of Syracuse, and the Free Library is an award-winning library located in the former Stickley Furniture factory. The boys and I were on our way to meet with Lauren Britton, a librarian at Fayetteville. She was going to show us how 3D printing worked.

A few months earlier, Sue Considine, the director of the Fayetteville Free Library, had announced to great fanfare the creation of a Fab Lab at the Library. Community members would be able to work with 3D printers and, eventually, other computer-aided manufacturing equipment. Lauren Britton had dreamed up the idea while a graduate student studying librarianship, and she and Sue were now making it a reality.

For my visit, Lauren had set up the 3D printer, a MakerBot Thing-o-Matic,[52] in the community room. It is a rather awkward looking box, about 2 feet in all dimensions. The MakerBot is not a high-end 3D printer—those sell for hundreds of thousands of dollars and are used by specialized manufacturers around the world. The MakerBot is an open

---

[52] http://www.makerbot.com (accessed May 8, 2012)

source machine that costs less than $2,000 and has grown quite a fan base amongst the "Maker" community. Connected to the printer was a laptop.

Over the next hour, she walked my boys and me through how the printer worked. We could come up with our own design or download something to print from thousands of premade models available through the web. We started with a ring. A simple ring that Andrew would later take in to his third-grade classroom bragging about how he made it at the library. Riley printed out a robot.

While the MakerBot is limited to printing items that can fit into a cube about 10 centimeters to a side, it shows an amazing potential of what is to come. Imagine if the next time you needed a part, or had an idea for a new gadget, or even wanted to create a replica of your favorite statue,[53] you simply printed them out. Not good at 3D design? Simply take a few pictures of a 3D object,[54] or spin it in front of your Xbox Kinect,[55] and send the resulting model to the printer. This is not science fiction; it is happening right now.

While it may not be science fiction, the question for us to ask is: why is it in a library? This is not a rhetorical question either. It is one that was asked by the Fayetteville Free Library Board of Trustees, some librarians at the library, and a ton of Internet readers when the announcement of the Fab Lab made the rounds on tech sites.

Rather than jump into that answer, I would like to broaden the question even further. After all, I just spent a chapter saying that libraries are not about books—so are they about Fab Labs? If we should no longer limit our definition of the library to collections and materials, how do we define a library? If I should expect more than book warehouses from my library, what should I expect? What does a library do?

Library as Facilitator

In a word, what libraries and librarians do is facilitate.

I realize to some that might seem anticlimactic. Revolutions in Egypt, Fab Labs, and being a beacon of community aspirations seem to call for a stronger word, like "empower," "advocacy," or "inspire." And libraries should do all of these. Recall that facilitation is only one part of the larger mission to "improve society through facilitating knowledge creation in their communities." The word improve is key. Improve is active. This means that facilitation is also active. To facilitate is not to sit

---

[53] http://gizmodo.com/5888230/the-smithsonian-turns-to-3d-printing-to-share-their-collection (accessed May 8, 2012)

[54] http://www.123dapp.com/catch (accessed May 8, 2012)

[55] Zollhöfer, M., Martinek, M., Greiner, G., Stamminger, M., Süßmuth, J. [leresistant] (2011, February 9). *3D face scanning with Kinect* [video file]. Retrieved from http://www.youtube.com/watch?v=llNSQ2u2rT4&feature=related

back and wait to be asked…no one ever changed the world waiting to be asked. No, you should expect the facilitation of librarians and libraries to be proactive, collaborative, and transformational. Libraries and librarians facilitate knowledge creation, working to make you and your community smarter.

They do this in four ways. Libraries:

1. Provide access
2. Provide training
3. Provide a safe environment
4. Build on your motivation to learn

I alluded to at least some of these when talking about libraries as safety nets. Each one of these means of facilitation can be seen as a sort of divide that must be bridged in order to learn. You have to have access to knowledge. Once you have access, you have to understand how to use it. Once you can use it, you must feel safe using it. Lastly, even if you have access and knowledge, and feel safe, you have to want to use the knowledge.

All libraries do the first aspect of facilitation, providing access. All libraries seek to do all four, at least nominally. Where too many libraries fall short is in how they: see knowledge as a thing, overemphasize access, and support consuming knowledge instead of creating it. If our libraries are going to support our communities in the future, they must do a better job across this spectrum.

What is Knowledge?

It would be easy to take those means of facilitation and add "books" or "databases" or any form of stuff to the end. For example, provide access to books/databases/materials. Too many libraries do this. However, that is not what I mean. I mean providing access to *knowledge*, and that is a very different beast than resources, books, and articles.

Here is what knowledge is not: it is not a passive and calm accumulation of facts. It is not a database of articles, or, indeed, a building full of books. It is not measured in pounds or linear feet. Knowledge is not static, not dispassionate, and definitely not cold.

Knowledge is something innately human and intimately tied to the passions of the individual. Knowledge is dynamic, ever changing, and alive. Knowledge drives us to question the world, to question each other, to question God, to question the nature of reality. Knowledge is a force that drives economies, drives art, and should drive librarians to service.

Knowledge is constructed in our libraries, our universities, our homes, our bars, and our cars. Knowledge is ultimately the way in which we see the world, and knowledge determines how we act.

The view of knowledge as dynamic and constructed is important when you talk about expecting more from libraries. Put simply, if you see knowledge as contained in books (and databases, and articles), then you facilitate the creation of new knowledge by collecting books and making them easy to get to. However, if you see knowledge as something more dynamic, and ultimately constructed by the individual and community, you need to radically change what a library does—you need to see the library as an active learning space.

This dynamic view of knowledge and learning is changing how we teach children in schools. Gone are the days when the "sage on the stage" model of learning was seen as the best form of curriculum delivery. Now, students co-create knowledge, get hands-on experience, and work on projects. We also see this in industry training. Hour-long PowerPoint sessions are being replaced with simulations and games. Cognitive and learning sciences are showing us that people are not empty buckets waiting for some skilled orator to fill them with knowledge. Rather, learners are active, constantly relating new ideas and facts to what they already know. The sage on the stage has been replaced by the guide on the side. Our libraries must go through this transition as well.

This new understanding of knowledge as actively constructed is perhaps the biggest expectation change we need to make in order to get the libraries we deserve. If I am to increase my knowledge, the library must allow me to do so actively. Certainly, in some cases reading about something is enough, but in many more cases you need to practice, and try, and explore to learn.

Buffy Hamilton, the librarian at the "Unquiet Library" in Creekview High School in Canton, Georgia (outside of Atlanta), knows this. Buffy doesn't spend much time organizing and shelving books. She is busy co-teaching projects like Media 21 that she describes this way:

"The school librarian and sophomore English teacher collaborated to create a semester-long participatory learning experience using social media and cloud computing to cultivate collective knowledge building and inquiry. Using tools ranging from Netvibes to Evernote to Google Sites, students blogged, contributed to group wikis, used social bookmarking, developed learning/research portfolios and presented learnings in a way that demonstrated an ethical use of information and licensed media. The program also was evaluated in terms of meeting Georgia Performance Standards and the American Association of School Librarian's Standards for 21st Century Learners."[56]

---

[56] http://theunquietlibrarian.wordpress.com/2011/01/05/ala-oitp-recognizes-the-unquiet-library-and-media-21-for-cutting-edge-technologies-in-library-services/ (accessed May 8, 2012)

And Buffy is hardly alone. Sue Kowalski is the librarian at Pine Grove Middle School in East Syracuse, New York. In 2011 her library was named National School Library Program of the Year by the American Association of School Librarians. Why? Not because of its collection or its architecture, but because of the learning students are doing and how that learning is tied into every corner of the school. Sue doesn't shelve books. Instead, she has created an "iTeam" of students who take care of the collection—and learn, and teach new technologies, and troubleshoot technologies for the teachers, and even organize events in and outside of the library.

How do good school librarians—the kind of school librarians you should expect to find in your school—connect and improve learning? Joyce Valenza is the librarian for Springfield Township High School outside of Philadelphia. She has developed a whole manifesto[57] on the topic. What should you expect from a school librarian in terms of reading?

- *You consider new ways to promote reading. You are piloting/ supplying learners with downloadable audio books, Playaways, Kindles, iPads, Nooks.*

- *You share ebook apps with students for their iPhones, droids, and iPads and other mobile devices (Check out Gale's AccessMyLibrary, School Edition)*

- *You market, and your students share, books using social networking tools like Shelfari, Good Reads, or LibraryThing.*

- *Your students blog or tweet or network in some way about what they are reading*

- *Your desktop screensavers promote great reads, not Dell or Apple or HP.*

- *You link to available free ebook collections using such tools as Google Books, International Children's Digital Library (See ebook pathfinder.)*

- *You review and promote books in your own blogs and wikis and other websites. (Also Reading2.0 and BookLeads Wiki for book promotion ideas)*

- *You embed ebooks on your websites to encourage reading and support learning*

- *You work together with learners to create and share digital booktalks or book trailers.*

---

[57] Valenza, J. (October 2012). Manifesto for 21st century teacher librarian. http://www.teacherlibrarian.com/2011/05/01/manifesto-for-21st-century-teacher-librarians/ (accessed May 8, 2012)

In terms of communication and publishing?

- *You know that communication is the end-product of research and you teach learners how to communicate and participate creatively and engagingly. You consider new interactive and engaging communication tools for student projects.*
- *Include and collaborate with your learners. You let them in. You fill your physical and virtual space with student work, student contributions—their video productions, their original music, their art.*
- *Know and celebrate that students can now publish their written work digitally. (See these pathfinders: Digital Publishing, Digital Storytelling)*

Note the active and collaborative voice. If you read the whole document (which I strongly recommend), you will see that this is a very different model of learning from the sage on the stage. A good school librarian is not a clerk or limited to maintaining a collection. He or she should be an active partner in learning. A good school librarian is a teacher who helps the subject area teachers improve. This librarian—the librarian you should expect in your schools—guides students through inquiry-driven learning free from the confines and limitations of too structured, too test-driven, too one-way "teaching."

What are the benefits of having this in your school? It turns out that you get well-documented increase in retention of students and higher test scores. Studies in Alaska, Colorado, Florida, Indiana, Massachusetts, Michigan, and North Carolina all showed higher achievement on standardized tests with the presence of a certified school librarian. One Pennsylvania study found:

"The mere presence of a large collection of books, magazines, and newspapers in the school library is not enough to generate high levels of academic achievement by students. Such collections only make a positive difference when they are part of school-wide initiatives to integrate information literacy into the school's approach to standards and curricula."[58]

These increases in performance do not come from simply having a room called a library in the school building. They are not tied to the size of the collection. They come down to one variable: the presence of a qualified school librarian. However, not just any school librarians will do. They must be engaged. They must be co-teaching and working with students on learning, not just focused on the materials.

---

[58] Research Foundation. (2008). School libraries work!. Retrieved from http://www.scholastic.com/content/collateral_resources/pdf/s/slw3_2008.pdf

Let me put this as plainly as I can: if your school does not have a school librarian, you are at a documented risk of lower performance. You should expect more from the school. If you have a school librarian and don't know his or her name? Expect more of that librarian. If you are a teacher and don't know how the library and librarian can help you in your classroom, expect more and demand an answer to that question from the librarian. If you are a principal and see the library only as an extended study hall or as a place to sink book-buying dollars, you need to expect much *much* more.

Expanding the Definition of Facilitation

All this emphasis on learning may make sense in a school library, but what about all libraries? Let's go back to our original question: what constitutes a library service? Let us take a look at those means of facilitation again, but this time let's add some definitions based on our more dynamic sense of knowledge.

Provide Access

The classic view of providing access is providing access to collections. This has been updated a bit to talk about access to information, but even information is often functionally defined as collections of texts, pictures, and materials, either digital or printed. There is a big problem with this view of access—it's one way only. In essence, too many libraries have defined access as providing access to their stuff. You must expect more from your library. You need to expect it to provide a platform where you can access the ideas of others, as well as a platform for you to provide others access to your own ideas.

Joan Fry Williams, librarian and prominent library consultant, put it best when she said that libraries must move from grocery stores to kitchens. A grocery store is where you go to consume, to buy ingredients for your meals. A kitchen, however, is where you go to combine these ingredients with your own skills and talents to make a meal. Kitchens tend to be social spaces, the place where everyone ends up at a party because it is the place where there is action occurring. Libraries need to be kitchens—active social places where you mix a rich set of ingredients (information, resources, talents) into an exciting new concoction that can then be shared.

This is what Joyce Valenza was discussing in her manifesto when she talked about things like students publishing their stories and collaborating with teachers and peers. Her library provided access not simply to materials, but to peers, teachers, community ideas, and tools like video cameras, laptops, social media websites, books, etc. Notice, however, that it was not the provision of tools that made Joyce's library a library; it was access to knowledge and the community itself. The tools of that access will change (from books to eBooks, from telephones to Skype), but the goal of access does not.

If your library is simply a place where you can go to consume—to get the publications and stuff of others—and not a place to create and to gain access to the rest of your community, you must expect more.

So how can a library facilitate knowledge creation through providing access? Well, in Fayetteville it was access to 3D printers, among other things. In academic libraries, it may be helping to organize study teams or building online communities. For example, group work is an increasing component of university-level teaching these days. Students are put into groups because the work they are being prepared for is collaborative and interdisciplinary. However, these teams are too often left to their own devices with little thought to how they can collaborate. Does the class provide access to online tools like discussion forums, tools to collaboratively edit documents, or places to archive online materials like citations? The library can and should be providing this type of active access. The library should be a place you go, either physically or online, to help you get at ideas and to help you share your ideas with others. That is how communities learn—through collaboration and conversation.

Of course, this assumes folks know how to get online or publish their ideas…

Provide Training

There is a fabulous video on YouTube titled "Medieval Helpdesk."[59] It shows a man from tech support explaining to a medieval monk how to use a book. He goes through the basics, like how you have to open the book and then turn the pages. No, the text doesn't go away when you turn the page; it is stored. To turn off the book you simply close the cover. Like any good joke, it loses its humor when explained (go watch the video), but it does challenge the idea that we are somehow born with the knowledge of how to use books. In fact, society spends quite a huge sum of money teaching people how to use a very basic technology like books. We call it reading.

All technologies need some basic instruction in how to use them. We don't learn to read by sleeping on top of books (as I discovered in 6th grade). Access is not enough. We must expect our libraries to help prepare the community to engage in active learning.

---

[59] Norwegian Broadcasting Corporation [nrk] (2007, February 26). *Medieval helpdesk with English subtitles* [video file]. Excerpt from *Øystein og jeg* [Television series]. Retrieved from http://www.youtube.com/watch?v=pQHX-SjgQvQ

So we now come to our second form of facilitation: providing training. Libraries should work with a community member in a learning activity specifically to allow that community member to engage in a larger conversation or larger learning activity. Many libraries do this already. In public libraries, librarians provide classes in basic computer skills and resume writing. For decades, academic libraries have been providing training in finding and using information (once referred to as bibliographic instruction—now more often simply called instruction). My favorite story about training comes from a law library.

A lawyer pops his head into the librarian's office, telling her that he has been searching all night for a piece of information on an opposing expert witness. He is due in court within the hour. Can the librarian help? Five minutes later, the librarian is printing out the needed information from LexisNexis. Now, we could stop here and have a heartwarming "librarian saves the day" story, but that is nothing new to libraries. Librarians have been providing reference services like this since the early 1900's. What makes this story great comes in the realization the librarian had and what she did about it.

The lawyer was looking for information about an expert witness. Lawyers call scientists, engineers, doctors and a whole host of experts to help them make their case. If a lawyer is trying to prove a defendant insane, they call a psychiatrist. Lawyers looking to prove a chemical unsafe call a chemist, and so on. This means that the character and expertise of that witness is very important. So lawyers who call the expert want to be sure of their credentials, and the opposing counsel wants to find some piece of information that can cast doubt on those credentials. This often involves discovering the witness has changed position on a topic, or finding some piece of contradictory evidence once published.

The law librarian saw that, although lawyers are experts in the law, finding and discrediting expert witnesses is ultimately an information problem and a different skill set. Lawyers weren't experts in chemistry or psychology and didn't know how to look for individuals who were refuting information or even where that refuted information might be found. Librarians, on the other hand, do. Now here is the masterful part. The librarian didn't simply go from lawyer to lawyer telling them she could help or that she was better at finding this information. She realized nobody likes hearing they are not good at something or that they can't find everything they need through Google. So she set up a class called (I love this) "Character Assassination 101."

In the class, she talked about sources to find academic articles, how to search for scientists in a given domain, and so on. After every example, she would add "or if you are busy, I could do that for you." Her usage shot up. Lawyers now knew how to better find this information and they saw someone who understood their problems and could help. If your librarian doesn't have a clue what you do in your organization—expect more.

There are plenty of examples of great library services in training, and they are not all simply seating learners in a classroom. For example, in Delaware, the state's Division of Libraries teamed up with government offices in economic development and adult education to build training centers focused on job creation and skills development:

"This grant will make a huge difference in being able to bring much needed mobile technology to our libraries, and offer Delawareans new services that will help them get ready for jobs, find jobs and enhance their education," said Governor Jack Markell. "While our libraries do a terrific job with information, these new services will make our libraries an even more valuable resource for people trying to equip themselves for a changing job market."[60]

Just about every public library in this country provides support to job seekers. However, this is often access to online job sites and access to computers on which to write resumes and submit job applications. In Delaware, they raised the bar. It is not enough to provide access; one must instill skills and education.

You will recall the northern Illinois libraries that banded together to create Transform U from Chapter 2. These librarians created partnerships with local community colleges, state workforce offices, and local businesses to provide one-on-one help in developing interview skills. A librarian will sit down with someone to walk through a college application. Through Transform U one can easily bypass red tape to talk to social services or find an internship.

These ideas extend into academic libraries. In place of bibliographic instruction, great libraries are now introducing a suite of concierge services. At several universities, freshmen are assigned a librarian upon admission. While colleges have always provided advisors to help students navigate a course of study, the librarian advises the student on the whole college or university information environment. Librarians meet with freshmen to go over their classes and talk about what resources will be helpful in those classes. They also cover the information systems students will be encountering, from course registration to dining plans to how to send email. Librarians, who cover all the disciplines on campus, can now help students see the bigger picture.

Academic librarians should not stop there. More and more academic librarians are embedding themselves in classes and departments. Subject

---

[60] http://governor.delaware.gov/news/2010/1009september/20100928-broadband.shtml (accessed May 8, 2012)

specialists from the library monitor Twitter feeds from classes and provide on-the-spot help. If a professor forgets a citation or a date, he or she can simply tweet out a question, and the librarian tweets back a response. Librarians now have office hours where they go into the departments and work directly with faculty on teaching and research as part of a team. They provide training not just in case a student or faculty member needs it, but at the point of need.

If your library—public, academic, school, government, corporate, what have you—is not in the training business, or that training is not aligned to what you are doing, when you are doing it, and where, expect more.

Provide a Safe Environment

Abraham Maslow was a professor of psychology. He knew a thing or two about training and learning. He knew, for example, that the environment in which people learn matters. He created what we now call Maslow's Hierarchy.[61] The Hierarchy argues that in order to learn, you need to have some basic needs met first. For example, you are going to have a hard time learning physics if you have no food to eat or shelter to protect you from the elements. Maslow called these physiological needs. Likewise, if you have food and shelter but no sense of safety, there is no learning. Maslow called these safety needs. His hierarchy continues to a need for belonging, esteem, and, finally, self-actualization. For our purposes here, I am simplifying things and focusing on the need to feel safe.

I started this book with the Arab Spring. Many credit social networking sites like Twitter and Facebook with bringing about mass protests and change in Egypt. However, what is not talked about nearly as often is that these same tools can be used to track and suppress protests. Voice of America, for example, reports on how the government of Bahrain is using Facebook to find and arrest protestors:

"Unlike in Egypt, however, the demands of the Bahrainis were never met. The Sunni government, with military help from neighboring Gulf States, quelled the uprising and afterwards, reportedly used access to social media to help identify and punish those who spoke out."[62]

Authorities from the Iranian government, to the CIA, to the San Francisco Police Department are turning to social network sites to identify potential social disruptions and stop them. Sites like Google and

---

[61] http://en.wikipedia.org/wiki/Maslow's_hierarchy_of_needs (accessed May 8, 2012)
[62] http://www.voanews.com/english/news/middle-east/Facebook-Becomes-Divisive-in-Bahrain-127958073.html (accessed May 8, 2012)

Twitter are adjusting policies to allow greater control by authorities. It may be that we have seen our last Facebook revolution as protestors seek the next safe haven for coordinating action.

Physical Safety

Safety comes in many flavors: the two that most concern libraries are physical safety and intellectual safety. Public libraries are often cited as safe havens. Latch-key kids, for example, can go to the library and stay off the streets. This was so important to the citizens of Philadelphia that when the mayor sought to close 11 branches of the library, the citizens and city council sued in court to keep them open. While there was talk of Internet access and knowledge centers, the reason cited, overwhelmingly, was that the community wanted a safe community space for kids.

This idea of providing physical safety is not limited to public libraries. School libraries often become havens for students who don't fit into other social groups. Academic libraries are safe places for undergrads to study late into the night or even to escape harassment from dorm mates. As Maslow pointed out, the physical environment matters. So can we expect more from our libraries than a guard at the door? This question was taken on by the Central Library of Philadelphia.

The Free Library of Philadelphia's Central Library had a problem with homelessness. Every morning before the library opened, the homeless of the central city would congregate in a park in front of the grand Beaux-Arts building. Once the doors of the Library opened, the homeless would crowd in to use the bathrooms and find a place to rest. Things came to a head when a board member of the library complained about the condition of the bathrooms after attending the Library's world-class lecture series.

The librarians of the Central Library had a choice to make. How were they going to deal with the homeless? They reached out to the city and other urban libraries for advice and help. Much of the advice the librarians received had to do with keeping out the homeless: policy changes they could make, laws they could use, and so on to "minimize" the problem. The librarians of the Free Library chose a different path.

The first thing they did was to hire homeless men and women to be bathroom attendants to keep the bathrooms clean. Then the Library started a café. The café was a community-wide effort. Major funding came from Bank of America. The equipment was donated by Starbucks. The food came from a neighborhood bakery. The café was staffed, trained, and managed by formerly homeless men and women now in a program to transition to work.

This is what happens when the public, or in this case, the librarians, expect more of themselves and their community. They look at people not as problems but as community members who are in need of services, support, and literacy and, ultimately, in need of power—the power to support themselves and live dignified lives. The power to create and learn, not simply to survive. Did the Free Library of Philadelphia solve the homelessness problem in Center City Philly? No. Instead it decided not to stand by and ignore it. It did not "minimize the problem." It leveraged the power of the homeless to deal with the problem, which the librarians had previously been powerless to address.

We will return to the physical building and how it can be not only safe, but inspiring later when we talk about communities in Chapter 6. For now, let me turn to another type of safety.

Intellectual Safety

For centuries libraries have been champions of intellectual safety. Librarians long ago realized that just as you need to feel physically safe to explore and learn, so, too, must you feel safe in your thoughts. If you feel someone is censoring ideas, or watching and judging the types of information you are looking into, you will be less likely to look into controversial subjects. This "chilling effect" is roughly equivalent to that feeling you got watching R-rated movies with your parents when you were 15.

Perhaps the most extreme example of libraries as guardians of intellectual safety came in the court case Library Connection v. Gonzales. Under the Patriot Act, passed after the 9/11 terrorist strikes, the FBI could get the records of libraries and other businesses in the process of investigations. This, on its own, was not new. The FBI had always had the right to subpoena such records. What was new was that now the FBI didn't need to go to a court to get the records; it could issue so-called National Security Letters on its own. What's more, unlike with the subpoena where a library (or a video store, or a school) could challenge the request in court, the letter came with a gag order, meaning you couldn't even tell anyone you got the letter, much less challenge it. The logic behind this change was to speed investigations and prevent tipping the hand of law enforcement.

The majority of librarians did not like these provisions in the Patriot Act. Librarians had made the privacy of library user information paramount for decades, fearing a chilling effect. In other words, if library users felt that what they read or what they looked at on the Internet was being monitored, they would self-censor. Librarians hold that the best knowledge is developed from the broadest array of sources. Library users had to feel sure that what they were looking at wasn't being monitored or judged. To be clear, intellectual safety is not about having library users look only at safe information; it is about library users feeling safe to engage with very challenging ideas.

With the Patriot Act, librarians could no longer assure the community of their safety. In 2004, a Connecticut group of librarians felt that things had gone too far in the balance of civil liberties and law enforcement, and they decided to do something: they sued when they got a National Security Letter, knowing full well that they might go to jail for doing so. Apparently the courts, including the Supreme Court, agreed that the balance was out of whack. The gag order was invalidated.

I don't tell this story as some morality tale against the Patriot Act. Rather, I want to show that libraries: 1. hold (or at least should hold) your intellectual safety very dear, and 2. can do so within the parameters set up by the community. The Connecticut librarians didn't let the person under investigation know about the National Security Letter in a hushed conversation in a darkened parking garage. The librarians didn't simply ignore the law. No—they went through the courts seeking not to gain some unique privilege for themselves, but to restore a long-standing balance between disclosure, privacy, civil liberties, and free speech. Libraries still have to give library user information to law enforcement, but only with judicial oversight.

While I don't think we can expect much more from librarians than risking jail to uphold the Constitution and ensure the community's right to explore ideas and, we can expect libraries to extend their ideals beyond the walls of the library. For example, most libraries go to great pains to keep what you do at the library private. Libraries work hard to eliminate Internet browsing history after each use. Libraries purge circulation records and do not track the books you are looking for. They do a pretty good job (I might argue too good of a job) of getting rid of your history within the library and library systems. However, when was the last time your library let you know that every click and keystroke you use to search for library books from home can be captured by your Internet Service Provider (ISP)? Do they let you know that you may be using an "anonymized" computer in the library, but by logging into Facebook your Internet browsing can be tracked by the social network company...even when you are not on Facebook?

Today, the threats to your privacy come not from Big Brother (the government), but from thousands of "little" big brothers. Facebook, Google, Twitter, banks, and insurance companies have spent millions upon millions of dollars to track what you are looking at, where you are, and what risks you represent.

Alexis Madrigal wrote about this in the National Journal:

"There's nothing necessarily sinister about this subterranean data exchange: this is, after all, the advertising ecosystem that supports free online content. All the data lets

advertisers tune their ads, and the rest of the information logging lets them measure how well things are actually working. And I do not mean to pick on The New York Times. While visiting the Huffington Post or The Atlantic or Business Insider, the same process happens to a greater or lesser degree. Every move you make on the Internet is worth some tiny amount to someone, and a panoply of companies want to make sure that no step along your Internet journey goes unmonetized."[63]

If libraries need to be providing us access to these services and training us about them, don't they also have an obligation to let us know about threats to our privacy? Can't they represent the community voice in the public discourse on such issues? Expecting more from libraries means expecting them to be informed about threats to privacy on a global scale and having them actively working with the community to come to an informed level of consent on disclosure.

In Chapter 6 we'll see the importance of libraries in being proactive on issues of intellectual safety and the peer concept of intellectual freedom (the safety to seek information and the right to do so). For now, let us look at the last form of facilitation—and it is all about you.

Build on Your Motivation to Learn

To talk about motivation, I need to return to the Fayetteville Free Library. You see, while we were busy printing out the robot and the ring on the 3D printer, the librarian, Lauren, mentioned an upcoming open house for the Fab Lab that would include the 3D printer, making jewelry, and making things in Duct Tape…if she could find someone who made things with Duct Tape. Riley, my 11-year-old, said "I make stuff with Duct Tape," and before Lauren knew what was happening he was flipping though pictures of his creations on his phone.

"Great," said Lauren without missing a beat. "You could teach it." And he did.

Clearly, the experience at the Free Library also had an impact on Andrew because a week later my youngest said he had a great idea for this year's science fair. "I'm going to design the library of the future!" he declared. Within 10 minutes he had sketched it out on paper.

Twenty minutes after that, he and his brother were building the library in Minecraft, a popular game akin to Second Life, or SimCity. Sure, they could build it in Legos (Andrew later did), but Legos don't have working roller coasters and you can't invite your friends from around the world to walk through it. (There are, as I write this, over 23 million registered Minecraft users.)

[63] Alexis Madrigal, T. A. (2012, March 1). I'm being followed: How Google—and 104 other companies—track me on the web. *National Journal.* Retrieved from http://search.proquest.com/docview/928046856?accountid=14214

Figure 6: Library of the future in Minecraft designed by Andrew and Riley Lankes

The next Saturday, we took the library of the future on a disk to Fayetteville, and printed it out.

Figure 7: Andrew holding his Minecraft model of the library of the future, printed on the MakerBot Thing-o-Matic

Now, you might think this is the point when I start to talk about millennials, or the power of Fab Labs, but that's not what sticks out to me about this story. What sticks out to me is the motivation my sons had and how that was encouraged by the librarian. Sure, the 3D printing was cool, but that's not what hooked Riley. What hooked him was when Lauren asked him to teach the Duct Tape class. What got him hooked was when he came into the Fab Lab two weeks later and saw that the librarians had hung his Duct Tape Fab Lab sign on the door. What got Andrew hooked was sitting in front of the MakerBot while it printed during the open house, and getting to explain how it worked and what it was printing.

Identifying and sparking motivation to learn is the most important form of facilitation. Without it, no one is prompted to learn, and all the programs, services, and activities of the library are for naught.

There are many ways libraries can inspire community members and build their motivation to learn, create knowledge, and, ultimately, to improve society. However, one of the most powerful is to cede some control and authority over the library to the community itself. This is more than simply talking about an oversight board or committee. This is more than talking about the community ultimately owning the library by funding it through tax dollars or tuition. This is allowing co-ownership of library services.

The power of co-ownership is hardly limited to libraries. While my children were working on these projects, the university faculty I am on was looking for new models of teaching. One that is frequently discussed is the "flipped classroom." The one where students do homework in class and classwork at home. The one where students do project based work in class and listen to the lectures online. But in the middle of this discussion—in the middle of 3D printing—it hit me. I apologize to all those who find this obvious, and I could probably have said these words before, but it really hit home for me:

While we sit here and debate when we deliver our lectures, or how long they are, or in what channels, the real flip is already occurring. The lecture? The long-form or short-form oratory? That is not the point of this. No, the real flip is that faculty are losing control. The real flip is the change from us thinking we have the content and that we are just debating the delivery, to the truth that we need to relearn the content continuously right alongside our students.

That last bit, the relearning bit, is crucial. This is not simply ceding control or turning education into one long do-it-yourself project. There is value in good teachers and good researchers. They will always have a strong ability to guide. It is about realizing that truly co-owning a curriculum or library program requires constant reinvention, if for nothing else than applying it to new contexts. It is why the university model of researcher/teacher has worked so well for so long. It is in the disconnection of these two things that we run into breakdowns.

The same is true of our libraries. The Maker Space concept that the Fayetteville Library is trying to capture—a place to not just study something, but to create and hack—does not work unless all are involved—librarians, members, experts, children, parents—and understand that they are all learning at the same time. If a kid shows up and is trained and treated as a consumer, the Maker Space will fail. No $2,000 MakerBot can match the quality of store-bought Legos or toys. No, the trick is to show the child, or parent, or member that they are part of a learning process and discovering something new—even if it is only new to them. They have to be in on the truth that we are all just figuring this out as we go. And if we have it all figured out? Time to try something new.

I know there are long discussions to be had about the role of experts, the value of experience, and the pedagogy of well-known and new areas. I get that. I know I am oversimplifying here, but that is kind of the point. Those discussions of expertise and pedagogy need to be just that—discussions and conversations. They are messy, and there is a huge amount of ego riding on them. Yet if we don't open those conversations up beyond the faculty—beyond the librarians—then we have shut down a most remarkable opportunity for motivation and community member involvement. And if we shut down conversation we have failed in our mission. We need to expect more.

Teacher, Librarian, Tinker, Spy

If you take one thing away from this chapter, take this: you should expect your library to be a proactive facilitator of knowledge. There is an excellent chance you will ask: why is this a library and not a school? In fact, if you look at the four means of facilitation of knowledge, you could easily apply them to folks like teachers, journalists, even publishers. Certainly the mission of improving society through knowledge creation would apply across these professions. I would not disagree.

The short answer is that the means of facilitation do not uniquely apply to librarians and libraries, but how these means are applied do. Libraries are defined not by their buildings, but how they combine the mission, the means of facilitation, and, ultimately, a set of ethics and skills. I firmly believe that over time the fields of knowledge facilitators that include journalists, teachers, and publishers will grow closer. We'll return to that when talking about "The Facilitators" in Chapter 7. For now, we need to spend some more time on what exactly I mean by "improve society."

5. Improve Society: Expect Grander

Let me be clear: talking about libraries improving society does not include jackbooted librarians marching down the street forcing citizens to properly cite works and read only approved books. I say this because there are those in the library community who think that when one's mission includes "improving society," it implies a fixed and somewhat authoritarian vision of improvement.

This suspicion is not completely unwarranted. For a good part of history, libraries were seen (and run) as elitist institutions that promoted reading the "right" literature. The right literature was often defined as material approved by white, male land owners.

This elitism still shows up in some unexpected ways. There is still plenty of talk about libraries being authority sites that collect only high-quality resources, with "High Quality" normally being defined by the reputation of the publisher of a given work. Certainly, this is the perception of folks such as faculty, parents, and businessmen. If you want quality information, go to the library. The library is (or at least should be) a location to find quality information resources, but to fulfill its mission the library can't store only high-quality materials. There are two problems with storing only high-quality resources: universality and negative examples.

I've already touched on universality a bit. Can there ever truly be a universal definition of high-quality? When the President of the United

States makes a statement, is that automatically high-quality information? Ask someone of the other political party or the president of Iran. We could try and get around this question by talking about universally recognized processes or markers of importance. So while we may not agree with a president, we can at least see his statement as important, right? In science, rather than talking about truth or quality, we talk about peer review, a process where a given community deems some idea as worthy. This is a great approach and one I advocate, but it is not universality—it is a community-based definition of quality. Quality, it turns out, is like pornography…you know it when you see it.

Here's the second problem with the library as keeper of high-quality information: there are few places on this planet with a greater concentration of lies and untruths than a good academic library. Why? Because you need bad information to produce good knowledge. I know that sounds like an oxymoron, but stick with me for just a few more sentences. If you study evolution, you probably also read works on creationism—if only to disprove it. If you want to advance science, you often do so by disproving a previously held theory. History collections are filled with racist rants and skewed biographies. Education texts talk about dealing with "the retarded", and psychology texts can still be found talking about "hysterical women". You need this information to know your history and to track the progress of our knowledge of the universe.

Several years ago, the MacArthur Foundation funded research into credibility and youth.[64] Several authors (including myself) came to the same conclusion: K–12 public schools are potentially the worst place to teach kids about finding credible information on the Internet. Why? Because it is actually hard for students to access non-credible information. Teachers and school librarians can show kids good information, but in order to see negative examples kids have to go home where they often encounter bad content with no supervision.

I am not talking here about pornography, I'm talking about sites like MartinLutherKing.org. Not a typo. You see, the site is actually built and run by Stormfront, a white supremacist group. Of course you would never know that unless you clicked a little link at the bottom of the page. In schools, this site is most likely filtered out, but at home? Teachers and librarians can't bring up the site to show students how racist groups can use the Internet to manipulate the young and unknowing.

Now here's one to twist your mind a bit: in some communities and for some questions the Stormfront MLK website is high-quality information. That community is not just the racist sect, but in your community as well. High-quality? Imagine a reporter looking for examples

---

[64] Metzger, M. J., & Flanagin, A. J. (2008). Digital media, youth, and credibility. Cambridge, Mass: MIT Press.

of how hate groups use the web for recruiting. Stormfront is one of the best resources for that reporter. However, it is not the best site to send to an eighth grader looking for after school activities. In discussions of quality, context matters.

Ultimately, what constitutes improvement within society is a local definition. Is your library there to increase research, encourage economic development, improve the bottom line, improve testing performance, provide recreation, or most likely, do a combination of these things? The library's goals need to be aligned to the larger community.

Expecting More Than Pie and Prostitutes

In Ann Arbor, Michigan, the librarians have a suggestion box on their website. They asked members what would make the library better. One of my favorite responses was (I'm paraphrasing here): more pie and prostitutes. Probably a joke, but this response actually raises an important counterbalance to the jackbooted librarians with which I opened the chapter. The opposite end of the spectrum from authoritarian librarians dictating one vision of improvement is a sort of anything goes definition. There is danger in a consumer-driven approach run amok.

Throughout this book, I talk about expecting more out of the library, but for a moment I need to talk about how libraries and librarians need to expect more out of you. Seeing every community member as a consumer is expecting far too little of you. You are not a consumer or even a customer of a library. Most libraries will use the term "patron" when referring to the community. This is slightly better, but still brings up images of rich estate owners in Italy paying for oil paintings. I prefer the word member.

This is an idea I owe to Joan Frye Williams, a librarian and library and information technology consultant. While working with several public libraries to create strategic plans, the question of what word librarians should use to refer to you came up, and she had a crazy idea... "Let's ask them."[65] In an informal survey of library users the answer she got more than any other was "member." After all, "I have a card and I pay dues [in the form of taxes]." I like this term because it connotes co-ownership. Members of an organization don't just use the organization and leave. They vote, set policy, and help. In essence, they are part of the organization. You need to expect to be part of your library. You need to be part of the conversation of what improves society and how the library can contribute to that goal.

Further, you must expect more of that conversation and more of the library than simply identifying what is wrong with the community.

---

[65] http://www.newlibrarianship.org/wordpress/?page_id=1052 (accessed May 8, 2012)

Librarians are great problem solvers. They love problems. They love the challenge of a good reference question. They love the hunt of finding an item. They are born to serve and often because of that they focus on the problems of the community. Those problems are great, and that work is important.

However, we must never forget that our communities have aspirations and dreams. Though the diversity of our communities can make it difficult to agree on a single vision, we know it is possible. The library can bring our neighbors and colleagues and students and members together in a civil, safe, and inspiring space to dream.

A great dream has the power to move nations. A great dream has the power to transcend differences, problems, and challenges. A great dream lifts us up out of the routine and the weight of the everyday. A dream has the ability to point us forward and to improve society. That, ultimately, is the kind of services we need from librarianship—not to be constantly reminded of problems, but to be wrapped up in a dream of a better tomorrow.

Of the Community

You also must expect a library to do more than simply take a dream and make it happen. Great libraries help shape the vision itself. Notice I use the word "conversation" throughout this book. It is done intentionally, and when talking about how communities seek to improve themselves and the larger society. It is important to know why I use "conversation."

A conversation is a complex thing. It involves at least two parties. It involves the language used by these parties, but most importantly, it involves listening and talking. A conversation is an exchange of ideas where both parties are shaped by the conversation and shape the other conversants. Without this willingness to listen, conversations quickly devolve into monologues and shouting matches.

In the conversation about what makes the community better and about the role of the library in that aim, we should expect libraries to shape themselves and their services to that vision of a better community. This is nothing particularly revolutionary. For decades, we have been talking about customer-driven approaches. In technology, we talk about user-centered design and user experiences. We should expect more than simply being consumers or users of the library; we should expect to be members—helping to shape the library itself.

This means we should also expect libraries and librarians to shape the conversation of a better tomorrow. Libraries need to be "of the community," not simply "for the community." On one hand that means that they offer not generic services but services shaped to best meet local needs. It means that library collections need to be as much (or more) about locally produced knowledge and resources as about materials from and about other communities. However, it also means that, as a member of the community, libraries and librarians have a voice in the shaping of the vision for a better tomorrow and in how the library achieves that vision.

Let me provide a current example: eBooks. Something very interesting is happening as books migrate from paper to electrons. Most folks focus on things like feature sets (highlighting, sharing notes, being able to sync where you are in a book across devices, multimedia) or devices (eInk eBook readers, tablets). To be sure, these are some pretty major changes in how we think about and interact with books. But most people have missed a much more fundamental shift. As publishers have moved titles to the digital world, they have also changed their business model from selling books to licensing them.

I know business models are a lot less sexy than super-slim tablets, but here is why you should care. Even though you think you are buying a book for your device, you are not. You are agreeing to pay for the use of that book under a license. What's the difference? You get one set of rights when you buy something, and you only get the rights the owner of the eBook wants to give you under a license. For example, if you buy a physical book, you can lend it to a friend or even sell it to someone else. This is called the first sale doctrine, and not only does it create an amazing used market for textbooks in college, it is one of the pillars upon which libraries are built. If you buy a book, you can sell it, or lend it to a friend...perfectly legal. So can a library. However, you can't resell an eBook. Why? You don't own it.

When you got your new eReader, you probably clicked on what is called an End User Licensing Agreement. This is the pop-up that you see every time you create an account on a website. It is often pages long, and, if you are like the vast majority of "end users," you never read it. Notice that you don't have to do this when you buy gum at the store. That agreement was a license, and with eBooks it pretty much says what you can and can't do with an eBook.

How does this play out in real life? In July 2009, two years after Amazon put out the first Kindle, many people bought an electronic copy of George Orwell's *1984*. The problem was that Amazon didn't have the right to sell it. So what did Amazon do? It remotely deleted the book from every Kindle that had purchased it. Only after the fact did Amazon let customers know it had done this and offer a refund. One commenter compared it to Ikea sneaking into your house late at night to repossess a bookcase.

What Amazon did was perfectly within its rights, because all the owners of Kindles had agreed to Amazon's policies and didn't own the book in the first place—they had only paid for the use of the book under the conditions that Amazon had set up.

So what does this have to do with libraries and the conversation about improving society? There is a growing demand for eBooks from library members, and publishers are getting increasingly worried about how they can make money off of their titles. Imagine if you could go register your eBook reader with your local library and seamlessly download any title you wanted free of charge. Why would you ever buy another book? Instead of selling a bunch of copies of the books, publishers would sell one to your library and be done. So publishers are seeking to introduce "friction" into this process. That is, they want to make it easier to license it directly from the publisher than to get it from the library. And most publishers are refusing to license eBooks to libraries at all.

Those who are agreeing to work with libraries are doing things like restricting the number of times libraries can "circulate" the eBook. So after 26 people have read a Harper Collins title, the library must license a new "copy." Random House had a simpler approach; it just raised the price of eBook licenses for libraries by 300 percent. In the physical ownership world, when the new bestseller comes out, you and a librarian can walk into the same bookstore and buy the same book at the same price—you take it home, and the librarian puts it on the shelf. But in eBook land, you can pay $10, and the library, if it can even get it, would pay $30.[66] And remember, these are the publishers that are willing to talk to libraries. This has led librarians to ask whether libraries (public, academic, school, etc.) should be in the eBook business at all. Some in the library community have started boycotts.[67]

Why this long story about eBooks? Because there is no question that communities of all sorts want eBooks in libraries. However, if the library simply does the best it can to meet this demand, two things may happen. The first is that the community will be dissatisfied with the selection. Many of the titles they are looking for will not be available through the library because publishers won't license them. The second thing that might happen is that a community may greatly reduce the services available at the library because more money has to be spent on eBook licenses.

[66] Matt Weaver, of West Lake Public Library in Ohio, told me of an order for eBooks that cost $926.58 in February, and $2,299.74 two weeks later.
[67] http://www.cbc.ca/news/arts/story/2012/04/02/ns-south-shore-libraries-boycot-random-house.html (accessed May 8, 2012)

To be clear, I have an opinion on this matter, but I don't begrudge any company or industry trying to make a dollar. A number of industries, including libraries, publishers, travel agents, doctors, musicians, movie producers, and game makers, are in great flux and trying to find their place and business model these days. We should expect librarians not only to be aware of this issue, but to be well versed in it. We also should expect the library to actively inform and help shape a community's view on this topic.

As with the Freegal service I mentioned in Chapter 2, does our community want to spend our resources on eBooks that can disappear at any moment? More than that, does our community want to take a stand on this issue? If you are not pleased with the idea that Amazon, or Apple, or Barnes & Noble ultimately owns the things that you are paying for (and can delete them at any time), you should expect our library to aid the community in making that view known, and actively work to change it.

This same argument is now taking place in our universities around the issue of scholarly publishing. In Chapter 2, I showed you just a glimpse of the tremendous costs involved in licensing scholarly databases (note: licensing, not buying). Many universities are increasingly annoyed that the government funds a researcher to do a study, the researcher writes up the results, and then hands it over to a scholarly publisher for free, to include it in a journal. The scholarly publisher then charges libraries, scholars, and universities to "buy" the article back at escalating prices. What's more, since the library, university, or scholar doesn't own the work, they simply are buying the right to read it. If the university ever stops paying the scholarly publisher, the articles vanish.

This has led an increasing number of academics and librarians to seek alternative models of publishing. For example, there is a huge open access movement. In the open access model, articles are published on the web for free. The resources to edit and review the work come from either the author or from some association that acts as publisher.

How does your community feel about this topic? What do they want to do about it? Several large universities, like the University of North Carolina and Harvard, have passed policies that dictate all publications should be open access (with some exemptions, to be sure). While this is very much a conversation for faculty to have about peer review, criteria for tenure, and even the obligation of the scholar to participate in open debate of ideas, the libraries have a big role to play here. We should expect librarians to educate the community, talk about the risks and benefits, and help shape the conversation around open access and scholarly communication. Note that I didn't say the library should determine a policy and enforce it. The library should enter into a meaningful conversation with the community where the library is shaped by the needs and desires of that community, but the conversation is also actively shaped with knowledge and expertise.

Walled Gardens

EBooks raise another issue about expecting more from librarians in terms of educating and organizing our communities: walled gardens. Walled gardens are proprietary systems for housing and delivering content. For example, if you own an iPad or iPhone and you want to add an app, you have to go through Apple's App Store. Not every app can be added either directly to the device or to the App store, so Apple has nearly complete control of the apps that you can access.

This concept is being extended to content as well. For example, buying books for your Amazon Kindle. Barnes & Noble stores, which sell their own proprietary eReader, the Nook, now refuse to carry physical books if the eBook version is available only on the Kindle. In physical bookstores, this is not a problem because there are other places you can go (like a library or another bookstore). However, on your Kindle, you have only one source—you live in a walled garden. It may be beautiful and all you will ever need, but the walls are still there.

I have just spent a good part of this chapter on books digital and physical, yet I keep saying that we need to expect more from libraries than books. Libraries, and therefore their concerns for an improved society, are all about the community. Does this concept of walled gardens apply there as well? Yup.

There is a 50/50 chance that if you use the Internet, you use a social networking site,[68] and, if you do, there is a huge chance you are using Facebook. Facebook is a walled garden, but in reverse. Ever wonder why it doesn't cost money to use Facebook? Because you are the product, not the client. Unlike Apple or Amazon where you are restricted in what you can get from the garden, Facebook controls what groups can take from (or about) you in their walled garden.

What you look at, who you are friends with, even the photos you upload are owned by Facebook, and that information is then resold to advertisers and others. (Remember the example of governments monitoring social networking sites to predict protests?) Now, for the vast majority of us, including myself, the value we get out of Facebook is worth the cost to our privacy. The rub is that many in the community are not aware that they are paying such a price, and most of us get annoyed when Facebook exercises its rights to change the rules of engagement.

---

[68] Rainie, L. (2012). *The emerging information landscape: The 8 realities of the "new normal"* [PowerPoint slide 11]. Retrieved from Pew Internet & American Life Project: http://www.pewinternet.org/Presentations/2012/Feb/NFAIS--New-Normal.aspx

This is particularly galling to folks who try to delete their Facebook account and find that Facebook has reserved the right to keep all of the status updates, pictures, and such in perpetuity (and use them in targeted advertisements).

Grand Challenges

So I come back to what we should expect from librarians in the conversation about improving society. There are clearly many aspects to the dreams of a community: economic, spiritual, recreational, scholarly, and so on. What aspects should we expect libraries to contribute to most? Rather than try and make a huge list of the areas where we should expect libraries to make a substantial community contribution, I prefer to talk about Grand Challenges.

A Grand Challenge is a fundamental problem with broad applications, which is answered by a wide array of approaches. It is an aspirational goal set by a community that seeks to help define and prioritize a field of study without dictating strategies and solutions. A Grand Challenge also serves as an invitation to institutions, scholars, industry, and governments across domains to meet the challenge. One of the best examples of this approach can be seen in biology and the mapping of the human genome.

Starting in 1990, scientists from around the world sought to map every part of the human genetic code, some 20,000 to 25,000 genes.[69] Partners from universities, government, and private industries believed that knowing the basic building blocks of life could unlock new treatments for disease, reveal new truths about evolution, and ultimately expand the capabilities of drug makers, doctors, and researchers. Over a period of 13 years, new technologies were developed and new understandings of how humans work at the cellular level were unlocked. The fields of biology, medicine, pharmaceuticals, criminology, and other fields will never be the same.

Are there some equally great challenges that we can expect our libraries to engage in? What are the Grand Challenges of library science, and how can we all work together to improve society? To answer that question, a group of librarians and information scientists gathered in Dallas, Texas in April 2011. What they came up with was a series of themes revolving around the central concept of the knowledge infrastructure.

The knowledge infrastructure is a rich mix of people, technology, sources, and permissions. Like DNA, the knowledge infrastructure is essential to your daily life, and, like DNA, you probably don't think about

---

[69] http://www.ornl.gov/sci/techresources/Human_Genome/home.shtml (accessed May 7, 2012)

it. There are the obvious parts of the knowledge infrastructure, like your cell phone. Of course, calling them cell phones is a lot like talking about "dialing" a phone these days. Over 50% of adults in this country own a smartphone[70], a phone they can use to surf the web and update social network sites like Facebook and Twitter. There are also other parts of the knowledge infrastructure we are getting used to, for example the digital networks that now deliver everything from texts, to movies, to music.

There are also parts of the knowledge infrastructure that we are becoming more and more aware of, such as policies and laws that affect how the infrastructure works. These days, when you hear about pirates, they are equally likely to be from Somalia, or the suburbs where teenagers are downloading the Captain America movie over BitTorrent. There is a huge debate over who owns ideas and content and what citizens are allowed to do with it. This concerns our national knowledge infrastructure.

Some see it as the knowledge infrastructure being put in action when colleges and universities (and high schools) going online to deliver distance education. Some think of the knowledge infrastructure as the Internet, and some would include phone systems (which are, increasingly, the Internet). Some may add repositories of information like libraries and museums to the knowledge infrastructure.

However, here in the U.S. the knowledge infrastructure has become much more diverse and woven into our lives. Take something as simple as driving to work. There is an excellent chance the car you are driving is controlled by a computer. Many new cars these days use a computer to regulate gas in the engine, monitor a suite of sensors so that it can text you if there is a problem, monitor wireless signals to unlock the car, and shut down the engine if the car is stolen. There are probably also other computers embedded in the car doing things like talking to satellites, and determining where you are (GPS) and what music you are listening to (satellite radio).

Your car is driving on top of a road that may look like it did 50 years ago, but that similarity is only surface deep—literally. If you are driving in a major city, you are driving on smart roads. Sensors embedded in the asphalt can detect how many cars are traveling on a road and at what speeds. They do this so that the streets themselves can control traffic lights to avoid congestion. These sensors are also being installed in remote rural parts of roads so that if the road freezes, the road can call for salting, thus minimizing costs and impacts on the environment.

Perhaps you are driving on an interstate on the east coast, where you can drive through tollbooths without ever slowing down because an E-

---

[70] http://articles.cnn.com/2012-03-02/tech/tech_mobile_smartphones-majority-pew-gahran_1_smartphone-cell-phone-android-phone?_s=PM:TECH

ZPass RFID system automatically detects your car and debits the toll directly from your bank account. You may not think of wireless toll systems as "knowledge" infrastructure, but recently, such technology has been used as a data collector to supply evidence for use in divorce trials. Lawyers can subpoena the toll operators to determine exactly where you were and at what time you were there. And this is all while you are driving.

By one estimate, very soon every mile of road will generate a gigabyte of data a day. It is assumed that this number will become a gigabyte an hour. As there are nearly 4 million miles of highway in the U.S.,[71] that would be 3.4 petabytes of data per hour, or 28 exabytes per year. What's an exabyte? It's 10x10x10x10 megabytes. Five exabytes could store every word ever spoken by humans—ever. So 28 exabytes of data on U.S. highways generated every year—a lot of data just from driving will be lying around.

Once again, you may not think anything of this, but when you have all of this data from our daily actions being collected, things can get downright creepy. Charles Duhigg is an investigative reporter for the *New York Times* and wrote a book, *The Power of Habit: Why We Do What We Do in Life and Business*. He tells the story about how the data collected through all of these seemingly invisible networks and sources can be put to unexpected uses like helping Target, the retail chain of stores, determine when someone is pregnant.

Pregnancy is a time of great change in a woman's life, and Target wants one of the changes to be buying more things at their stores. Target uses all of the data it has on customers (What coupons have we sent them? Did they use the coupons? What email did we send them?) to better target (no pun intended) its marketing efforts. In a recent interview, Duhigg talked about how Target can figure out when a customer is pregnant:

"So one of the analysts - and I spoke to the guy who ran this program, who kind of built this model. One of the analysts figured out that women who start buying, all of a sudden, a lot of unscented lotion might be pregnant. And then they started looking at what else those women bought, and they were able to run these little experiments because they have a baby registry. So they have a whole bunch of people who they know are pregnant, who told them what their due date is.

And if you buy unscented lotion, and then all of a sudden you start buying certain vitamins like zinc or magnesium, then that means that you're probably pregnant, and you're probably in your second trimester. And if you wait a little while

[71] Kane, A. "U.S. highway system overview. Engineering and Technical Services For ICAF Meeting. March 10, 2006. Conference Presentation. Retrieved from http://downloads.transportation.org/Kane-2006-03-10.pdf

longer, and that same person starts buying washcloths and cotton balls and hand sanitizer, which they've never purchased before, then you can use this information.

And there's about 25 different products to figure out, within a two-week window, what that woman's due date is. So even if this person has never told you that they're pregnant, in fact maybe they haven't even told their parents that they're pregnant, Target, by looking at their shopping patterns, can figure out not only if they're pregnant but when their likely delivery date is, and that gives them an enormous power to send them coupons at precise moments."[72]

If Target can be so accurate, what else can you, your community, or others do with so much information—good and bad?

Now, here is the trick about our current knowledge infrastructure: it's broken. It may not seem like it. After all, our phones still work, the traffic lights get changed, and Target makes a buck, but it is broken.

To begin with, it is currently uncoordinated and often conflicted. While the infrastructure is, and will remain, a marketplace with a mix of public and private components, few policies exist to make it better. What's more, the knowledge infrastructure is greatly tilted in favor of a simplistic view of consumption and production. In this view, there are entities that produce content (books, movies, songs, etc.), and there are consumers who buy or acquire it. The problem is, this model does not make much sense any more. We are all producers and consumers. Even our cars are producers and consumers. We are participants in a conversation, not simply customers in a market.

Think about YouTube. It is a site where you can not only watch viral cat videos, but you can also add your own video. Now, take a look at the Internet connection you use to connect to YouTube. Odds are it is an asymmetrical line, which means that you can download information a lot faster than you can upload it. You can pull down that viral cat video in 10 seconds, but it might take you 10 minutes to upload it. Why? Because the assumption when allocating bandwidth is that you will consume a lot more than you produce.

This is true not only in technology, but in all aspects of knowledge infrastructure. Go to the library—check out a book. Easy, right? Now go back to the library and try to get them to shelve a book you wrote. Go to a college and take a class. Now go and ask to teach one. Or worse, go and propose to have a class with no teacher and just a bunch of students working on a project.

Where is it easy to put information into a knowledge system? Where that knowledge can be easily monetized. Now we're back to sites like Facebook that don't charge you because you are the product.

---

[72] http://www.npr.org/templates/transcript/transcript.php?storyId=147192599 (accessed May 8, 2012)

Now let me be clear: the reason we need a more participatory infrastructure is not because of some grand utopian vision of equity for all, though that would be nice. Think of it instead as a vested self-interest in entrepreneurship and innovation.

In rural New England, for instance, there was a man who loved snowmobiles. All his life he collected snowmobiles and snowmobile parts. He loved them so much that by the time he retired he had a barn full of old snowmobiles and parts. One day his grandson, who was on break from college, came for a visit. With the permission of his grandfather, the college boy went into the barn with a laptop and a camera. Within a week (and with the permission of his grandfather) the boy had the entire barn inventoried and online. Overnight, this barn was transformed into a worldwide parts distribution center. One of their biggest customers was Siberia, where there were a lot of old snowmobiles, but not too many parts for them.

Without a more participatory approach to our knowledge infrastructure, these unexpected acts of entrepreneurship become more difficult. This also applies to things like the walled gardens I talked about previously. Without a balance of the proprietary and the open, the knowledge infrastructure breaks down.

Is My Library that Grand?

What does this Grand Challenge tell us about how libraries can work within communities to improve them? To begin with, libraries have historically been a large part of this knowledge infrastructure. While they play a much smaller role today, they are still vital. You can start with the fact that 99.3% of public libraries offer free public Internet access and 64.5% of public libraries report that they are the only free provider of Internet access in their communities.[73] Furthermore, as local, state, and even the federal government are turning to the Internet as a means of doing business, libraries of all sorts are being called upon to provide access and support to the public. Where once there was some local governmental office available to help with problems, now you have a local library with PC and librarians to help.

Libraries play a substantial role in the knowledge infrastructure in other ways. For example, the Copyright Office of the United States of America is an office within the Library of Congress. This office doesn't simply register someone's ownership of a work; it sets policy as to what constitutes fair use and infringement of the copyright law.

---

[73] http://www.plinternetsurvey.org/analysis/public-libraries-and-community-access (accessed May 8, 2012)

From its website:

"The Copyright Office provides expert assistance to Congress on intellectual property matters; advises Congress on anticipated changes in U.S. copyright law; analyzes and assists in drafting copyright legislation and legislative reports; provides and undertakes studies for Congress; and offers advice to Congress on compliance with multilateral agreements, such as the Berne Convention for the Protection of Literary and Artistic Works. The Office works with the executive branch's Department of State, the U.S. Trade Representative's Office, and the Department of Commerce in providing technical expertise in negotiations for international intellectual property agreements; and provides technical assistance to other countries in developing their own copyright laws."[74]

When Google expanded its mission to make all of human knowledge available, it showed up at the doorsteps of libraries. Academic libraries hold a huge portion of the research record of the past millennia. This doesn't even take into account the role that libraries of all types play in educating the population on how to engage, use, and create knowledge. Suddenly, all those justifications for the library discussed in Chapter 2 take on an increased importance when put in the light of the knowledge infrastructure that represents a huge and increasing portion of our national economy.

Yes, the idea of the knowledge infrastructure is grand. You may wonder, can I really expect my local librarian to play a role? Yes. School librarians can be instrumental in the shift away from heavy static textbooks to more authentic ways of learning and a much more diverse pool of resources (including experts and other students). In fact, that is exactly what is called for in the new Common Core academic standards being adopted by many states. Today's schools are being asked to shift from teaching a body of facts and formulas to teaching inquiry and process. What better place to support students in learning through process than a library, whose basic mission is the process of finding and making sense of knowledge?

Academic librarians can advocate for open access to scholarly knowledge in order to increase the rate of discovery and exploration. Government librarians can provide citizens with easy access to the inner workings of government, bringing sunlight to our democracy. Corporate librarians can ensure the proper management of intellectual assets so that companies can improve their bottom line.

The future of our economy, our democracy, our education, and our daily lives is increasingly dependent on and interwoven with the

---

[74] http://www.copyright.gov/circs/circ1a.html (accessed May 8, 2012)

knowledge infrastructure. We need to expect our libraries to prepare us for participating in this infrastructure. If your library thinks itself too small to make an impact in this Grand Challenge—expect more. If your library treats you like a consumer or limits its vision to the assets under its roof—expect more. Your community is too big to fit in the confines of the library, but too important to not have the library acting as your advocate in the larger world. Expect more.

6. Communities: Expect a Platform

As you have figured out by this point, I am using community in a broad sense. I do not restrict the word to mean the public or a geographic locale. Communities are groups of people that have come together around some common variable. That variable may be where they live, or the school they attend, or the institution they work for. In all cases, I assume that members of a community are conscious of this variable, that they are deliberately part of a community. So if you attend or work at a university, that university is a community. If you pay dues into a membership organization like a club or professional association, that, too, is a community.

Note that you are not restricted to a single community. You may be part of a community at work, part of the community where you live, part of a community that is a professional association, and so on. Not all communities need libraries. But in the communities that do need them, the library is part of the community, and you should expect that library to have a voice in improving the community.

Communities have aspirations and dreams. You should expect the library to help refine and facilitate those dreams. Communities also have problems and challenges, and you should expect the library to not only help solve these problems, but to document the way it helps.

We also know a few things that communities should expect from their libraries. Libraries should be places for knowledge creation and sharing, not just consumption and checking out books. We know that the function of a library must transcend the boundaries of walls. Communities should expect libraries to provide service to our increasingly on-the-move population. That means that students should be able to access library services from home. Employees should be able to access their library from their smartphones. Citizens should be able to interact with the public library on the web, in community centers, and in city hall.

Library as Platform

The new view of the library is not as place, or as collection, but as a community platform for knowledge creation and sharing. This is more than just a rhetorical shift. It has real implications for how libraries organize themselves and how they use technology. Let me give you some examples.

Polaris Community Profiles

Polaris is a library software company (not affiliated with the ATV manufacturer—or the star, for that matter). It makes what libraries call Integrated Library Systems or ILS. This is the software that allows librarians to purchase new materials, organize them, put them on shelves, and check them out. It is, at its heart, an inventory control system. It matches perfectly a model of libraries as warehouses of stuff. That software you use to search for a book? ILS.

Polaris gets that libraries are changing, and it is seeking to change with them. So Polaris went about designing a community profile system. The idea is that librarians could add community information into the ILS. In other words, they could add organizations with relevant information such as hours, contact info, and so on. Now, you could search for a book on teaching adults to read and up would come information about literacy agencies in the community as well.

Then Polaris took the next step. Why not have the community organizations add their own information directly? After all, who is more familiar with the services of that organization, and who has a bigger stake in keeping the information up to date? Now local organizations could add their information and events and even use a set of pre-designed templates to create their own web presence expanding their audience to library members and housing their web presence with a trusted local source (that also provided training on running a website). Now, you could find out about a local children's foundation through the library's catalog, and the foundation would have a web address that would help it reach its stakeholders. What's more, the local organizations could add related library resources to their page or link to their own sites not hosted by the library. For example, a local technology incubator in Syracuse that had its own servers could embed links to county library resources, including million-dollar databases on companies, patents, and the like.

Polaris' ILS has become a platform that allows a community to share and discover services, and embed community owned resources (like licensed databases of articles for research) within their local organizations. What's more, once the ILS was populated with organizational events, the library could share information on community happenings with any community member for new applications never dreamed about (or developed) by the library.

One such application is an iPad app recently developed by a student at Syracuse University. The student plans to mount iPads on local buses. The iPads will determine your location and tap into the events calendar in the library's ILS, so riders can explore what is happening nearby.

Here is the library as a platform in action. The event information being used for the iPad app is not owned by the library. The app itself was not developed by the library. The location where the app and information are being used is not within a library. Yet without the library, this project would not be possible. Without a place (provided by the library) for the community to enter, store, and retrieve this data, the app simply would not work.

We can take this community profile system one step farther into the future. Imagine these local organizations are adding event information as part of their profiles. One kind of event they can add could be a class that they want to offer. Since it is a part of the library platform, the class' profile page can refer to what is going to be taught, who will teach it, and when, and it can also include library resources that will be used in the class. So a community member could discover a nearby class on her smartphone, register for it, and then get online readings and activities needed for the class, all in one place. With the addition of discussion tools and video streaming, this system could evolve into a full-blown course management system. Public libraries can truly become the university of the people by hosting open courses. But wait, there's more!

It doesn't take a lot of imagination to see this same system in a higher education context. A professor could use the community portal features to create his or her own course on the ILS of the college library. He or she would simply add the details of the course, and then, with a simple set of clicks, add readings, media, and tools to the class. Add in grading and quizzes and, voilà, course management. Why do this versus going out and buying a learning management system like Blackboard? Well, the college already has a technology infrastructure plus a staff trained to maintain the ILS. Why build a separate infrastructure and silo for delivering courses? There is the added benefit of putting course materials into the hands of college personnel that are best suited to archive the material over time, and promote interdisciplinary collaboration. Usage of materials would go up; investment in IT would be leveraged; students and faculty wouldn't have to learn multiple systems; and the ILS is already well integrated into college systems like student records and IDs.

Community Garden

Sometimes the platform the library provides has little to do with technology. In Cicero, New York, the library platform is built from the ground up—literally. Meg Backus is a librarian at Northern Onondaga Public Library (NOPL) and she is charged with developing programs like classes and events. To develop programs, Meg listens to the community. The community, it turns out, likes gardening. Or, rather, the community is interested in gardening, and wants to know more.

Rather than inviting some gardeners into the library for a talk, Meg decided, with input from the community, to do more. She brought together interested community members and they built a garden they called the LibraryFarm[75]. The community dug up and tilled a plot of soil next to the library. They divided the land into parcels, and people could "check out" a parcel for the season. Now folks with little gardening experience or without a yard could come and plant, and get advice from experts in the community. This led to a series of talks and demonstrations, and all of them were grounded (sorry about that) in doing. Once the crops came up, the excess harvest was shipped to local food pantries. What started as a discussion of gardening became an expanded platform for learning about nutrition, buying local, and a whole host of other lessons. What did it cost the library? Water from a hose.

Reorganizing the Research Library

I consulted with a large research library that was in the midst of reorganizing after an administrative death spiral. The dean of the library had been fired, morale of the staff was non-existent, and the provost had hired a new director to bring the library back to life. That new director had brought in consultants (including me), not to come up with a new plan, but to bless the one he had created (which was really good). The centerpiece of that plan was a reorganization of library staff, reports, and functions.

Most libraries are structured into two big sections: public service, which includes everything facing the community; and technical service,

---

[75] http://www.nopl.org/library-farm (May 8, 2012)

the back-office library operations. So when you walk in and browse the shelves, or check out a book, or talk to a librarian, you are using public services. The part you don't see, like buying materials, cataloging them, and maintaining the Integrated Library System, all fall to technical services. This model of library organization is so prevalent that you find it in most academic and public libraries in this country. It is so widespread you will also find it in Africa, Europe, and throughout Asia.

Why is this model everywhere? Well, a lot of it comes from how we educate librarians, and a lot of it comes from an increasingly outdated model of library as book warehouse. Technical services are where the books come in; public service is where they go out. But is this how your community works? Does this model match a more participatory view of communities?

In creating his plan, the new director took a look at one of his target audience: researchers. His was primarily a research-oriented faculty, but also included doctoral and graduate students, and advanced undergraduates focused on the discovery of knowledge. The director found that a researcher needs to consume a great deal of information at the start of a study. The researcher needs background materials, examples of previous studies, and access to new concepts and theory. At this stage, the division of public service and technical services still makes sense. But as the researcher progresses, it begins to break down.

For example, say a researcher gets external funding. Increasingly, as part of a proposal, researchers must lay out how they are going to collect data, how they are going to keep that data over a long period of time, how they are going to disseminate that data (not just published papers, but the actual collected data), and how they are going to secure any private information provided by people involved in that study. Libraries today actually have systems to do this. Normally such operations are in the back office: technical service. The back office is also where libraries create a website around a project, or store papers and conference presentations based on the study. Because the researcher only interacts with public services, he or she has a hard time getting the technical services he or she needs. The old division of what faces the community breaks down, because the researcher is both a consumer and producer of information.

This distinction between community-facing and back-office also gets cloudy when looking at the teaching functions of a college. The faculty may be consuming information in the form of papers and media to bring into the class. They are also, however, creating their own collections and unique materials. How do these member-produced items fit into the library? Currently they don't, and all this information sits on the hard drive of a faculty member who may or may not keep it, or may or may not leave it with the college when retiring or getting another job.

So, let's go back to the research library that hired me as a consultant. The library director threw out the technical services and public services model. Instead he organized his services by research and teaching. If a researcher came in, he or she met with an assigned research librarian. Together, they went over the project, and the assigned librarian would organize the services of the library around the faculty member's project. The faculty member didn't need to know, or care, that it was technical services that built a website for the project. The faculty member didn't need to know that it was the reference department that did a literature search on the topic, or that it was actually IT that maintained a secure hosted data store to protect research data.

Likewise, teaching faculty would meet with their assigned teaching librarian to go over instructional services the library could offer them, put materials on reserve for classes, and even request copies of textbooks to be added to the library collection.

The library in this case became a human platform for accelerating the strategic goals of the university: better research and better teaching. In this example, however, folks were expected to come to the library. What if the library embedded itself in the community?

eScience

In 2001 Ellen Roche, a 24-year-old lab technician, entered into a clinical trial at Johns Hopkins University's Asthma and Allergy Center. The trial was investigating how the lungs responded to chemical irritants. Researchers had Roche inhale hexamethonium. Roche was the third volunteer to do so in the study. The first volunteer had developed a slight cough that lasted a week. The second volunteer had shown no adverse reactions. Roche developed a slight cough that got worse and worse. Five days after inhaling the chemical, Roche was admitted to intensive care. Less than a month later, she was dead.[76]

What makes this story all the more tragic is that Roche's death could have been avoided. As part of the funded clinical trial, the researcher did a literature search. He searched a database that indexed studies from 1960 to the present day. He found nothing on hexamethonium. However, had he not restricted himself to the Internet-accessible version of the database he would have found studies from the 1950's linking hexamethonium to significant lung problems. Because of Roche's death, all drug studies at Hopkins must now include a consultation with a librarian and pharmacist.

This story is tragic to be sure. However, I fear death by lack of information is inevitable. You will recall the discussion of the broken

---

[76] Keiger, D. & De Pasquale, S. (2002). Trials & tribulation. John *Hopkins Magazine, 54*(1). Retrieved from http://www.jhu.edu/jhumag/0202web/trials.html

knowledge infrastructure. It is growing in size and complexity. Today's scientists are confronted by an increasing body of evidence in databases, a huge growth in data available for study, more complex problems that are requiring greater collaboration with researchers in other institutions and in other fields, and whole new platforms for scientific investigation. Take, for example, the search for the fundamental particles of the universe at the Large Hadron Collider in Europe.

The Large Hadron Collider is a loop of complex electronics and powerful magnets almost 17 miles long buried under the countryside in Switzerland and France. It has the ability to accelerate particles to nearly the speed of light and precisely smash them together. In the collision, the particles splinter and release fundamental particles like quarks and, hopefully, the so-called God particle, the Higgs boson that gives the universe mass.

The Collider cost approximately $9 billion to build over more than a decade of construction. Needless to say, you don't build one of these for each set of scientists or universities doing physics research. Scientists from around the globe collaborate either virtually or in person to work with the Collider. To give you a sense of just how complex it can be to support this scale of scientific research, one article published from an LHC experiment listed 3,046 authors.[77]

These forces of large data and wide-scale collaboration are not limited to physics. Humanities scholars can now dig through hundreds of thousands of digital texts as part of their work. Social scientists are analyzing billions of web pages and social media updates studying how we behave online. Pharmaceutical companies can now generate millions of possible chemical combinations to fight disease—each one needing to be explored to make sure a new drug can help you, not kill you.

To help accelerate science and avoid the potential disastrous consequences of information overload, a special corps of librarians is now being hired into laboratories. These librarians work directly with researchers to organize mountains of data, ease collaboration between virtual teams of scientists around the globe, and build tools to investigate a host of new questions. They are learning how to specialize their means of facilitation to the scientific endeavor. To facilitate access to the mountains of data being generated in labs, they use databases and the latest search engines. They also use work-group software and web conferencing to spread good ideas quickly among their teams. They provide researchers training on the latest collaborative tools and ways to seek out funding opportunities. They build a safe environment by

---

[77] ATLAS Collaboration (2012). Search for down-type fourth generation quarks with the ATLAS detector in events with one lepton and high transverse momentum hadronically decaying W bosons in sqrt(s) = 7 TeV pp collisions. Retrieved from http://inspirehep.net/record/1091070

ensuring the data is secure. They match the motivation of research staff by helping disseminate their work throughout the field.

While we can't expect every librarian to wrangle 3,046 scientists or bring order to a million points of data, we can expect librarians to go to the community. The community lives within and outside of the library, and so should librarians. From the sole librarian working in a small town to a medical librarian working in a hospital, you should expect your librarians to spend some of their time getting out of the library and into the community. Librarians should sit with faculty, sit on Chambers of Commerce, and be at workplaces, not wait for the community to come into the library.

Of course, there are times when it makes sense to expect the community to come into the library. We have just talked about embedding librarians within the community; what if we embedded the community into the library?

Dallas Public Library

I mentioned before that a number of libraries around the world were organized in a single way (public and technical services). It turns out they are physically laid out the same way as well. This is not an amazing coincidence. Libraries have been seeking standardization over the past century or so. These standards are ingrained in policies and even in the law. In Dallas, all branch libraries were built or refurbished around a master plan.

The Dallas master plan dictated the number of square feet, the number and placement of stacks, the location of the information desk, and so on. This leads to a sort of McDonald's-like familiarity. No matter where you go, you know what to expect. Except even McDonald's has realized that reflecting local culture builds a greater feeling of local investment.

Corinne Hill, director of the Dallas library system, realized this, too, and sought to shake up the master plan. In neighborhoods with a large artist community, she helped design libraries with gallery space and painting lofts. She worked with local developers to come up with libraries that reflected the community in look and feel. When talking about what these buildings had in common she said that she put collaborative spaces in the middle, and books around the outside, as if they were art. Now you might take that as a sort of dismissal of books as decoration, but that's not what art is for. Throughout history art has sought to inspire, to educate, to provoke, and to remind. The books were not there for decoration; they were there to fuel the real work of the library: facilitating collaboration.

She took one step further in designing her central library in downtown Dallas. On the fifth floor of the building was the Business &

Technology division. It was there to help people start, grow, and understand business. Corinne knew the community needed more, so she cleared out half the floor and replaced the stacks with work desks, white boards, and projectors. She wanted the space not only to refer to business but also help business grow directly. She invited in local start-ups and let them set up shop in the library. She encouraged her own staff working on new ideas and projects to set up shop there as well. She embedded the community within the library.

This model is not unique to Dallas. The Ann Arbor District Library has on staff a number of production librarians. Their job is to work directly with the community to produce new tools and projects. Someone comes in with an idea for a new website? The production librarians can help them build it. A video project? Production librarian. The library is a place for the community to create.

Eli Neiburger, an associate director for Ann Arbor who oversees the production librarians, told me about a great idea. A community member came into the library and asked if his books at home could be added to the library catalog so people could borrow them. The member was more than willing to drop off the books if they were requested and thought other people would share their materials as well. In the way we currently think of libraries, this is an odd idea. After all, members' books are not owned by the library. But when you think of the library as a platform, and a library being "of the community" instead of "for the community" it makes perfect sense. In fact, this pooling of personal collections is how many libraries in this country started.

But why stop at the community's stuff? Why not use the library as a place to share the entire community? Libraries around the globe are starting to loan out people. You can check out production librarians in Ann Arbor, or a 3D printing librarian in Fayetteville, and some libraries are loaning out firemen and lawyers and accountants. The community experts want to volunteer their time, and the library can help maximize their efforts. In Europe there are now prejudice libraries where community members can check out a prejudice. Never talked with a Muslim? A gay or a lesbian? A Latino? A Republican? Now you can. This works because the library provides a civic and safe space to have such conversations.

Libraries as Place

I have talked before about libraries as aspirational institutions. Communities large and small build libraries to be monuments as much as they build them to be functional spaces. Architects use libraries as portfolio pieces, rich in marble and mahogany. This is appropriate. The community should look at physical libraries as representatives of their highest ideals.

In the past, however, this has been, frankly, annoying. Libraries may be aspirational, but they still need to be functional. All those libraries that Carnegie built a century ago? Many have them have been abandoned or repurposed because they are too small or too inflexible for larger collections, wireless networks, and new services. There are many librarians who groan when an architect is hired because too many architects see a library as a beautiful showpiece for the community to pose in and not a place where work needs to be done.

However, that is changing. Why? The short answer is a new approach (detailed in this book) and Moore's Law. Intel co-founder Gordon E. Moore stated that either the number of transistors on a computer chip would double every two years or the cost of putting the same number of transistors in the chip would halve. Moore's Law, as his theory has come to be known, has held up over 40 years, has been used more broadly to talk about how technology doubles in capability or halves in price every two years. This can be pretty striking and has held up in study after study. A computer from 1982 weighs 100 times as much, is 500 times larger by volume, costs approximately 10 times as much, and runs 100 times slower than the average smartphone in your pocket today.[78]

How does this concept— of digital technology speeding things up and shrinking them down—play out in a library? Does the building get smaller? Of course not, but libraries of the past were infrastructure in which librarians would do their jobs. Today that infrastructure is getting smaller and smaller. Encyclopedias that used to take up shelf space are now searchable from a computer. Card catalogs that would take up substantial floor space are gone, now searchable on that same computer. Microfiche is scanned and on the computer.

This shrinking through technology has had big effects. The first is on the design of the physical library. Stacks of physical resources can now be compressed into smaller space, allowing robotic systems to retrieve them, like at the Joe and Rika Mansueto Library at the University of Chicago.[79] The books and physical items are stored underground on shelves 50 feet tall, and retrieved to a glass-enclosed dome above ground where the university community can meet and study. New building materials allow light to flood into libraries and make them innovative and inviting spaces.

The second effect has been on the librarians. Now the librarians can leave the building and facilitate knowledge. Most of their needed tools are available through tablets and smartphones. Libraries can recruit workers from all over the globe to aid in digitization, building web-based tools,

[78] http://en.wikipedia.org/wiki/Moore's_law (accessed May 8, 2012)
[79] http://mansueto.lib.uchicago.edu/shelving.html (accessed may 8, 2012)

and even providing question answering 24 hours a day because fast digital networks make telecommuting a reality.

This may lead you to ask, as many communities have, whether we still need the physical library at all. The answer is up to the community. As the librarians need less and less space to do their work, the community needs more and more space to interact and create. Physical library buildings are being transformed into a third space.

The third space is an idea put forth by sociologist Ray Oldenburg. The first space is where you live, your home. The second space is where you work, your office; and the third space is where you go to be part of a community. The third space can be a barbershop or bar. Throughout Europe it is often the piazza, the town square. The problem with the third space is that it is disappearing. Even in Europe, piazzas are either being redeveloped or over-regulated. In the U.S., many third spaces are actually commercial spaces. So yes, Starbucks is a third space, as is the shopping mall. But these are regulated spaces for commerce that can distort the types of interactions and conversations that can take place.

Remember the Dallas Public Library branches? One of them was going to anchor a neighborhood redevelopment. When the developer was asked why, without prompting he talked about Oldenburg's third space concept. He said he could build places to live, he could mix it with places to work and shop, but he needed a place for the community to come together and develop identity. For him, that was the library.

This concept is not just about public libraries, either. Universities are finding they need a place beyond the dorm and classroom. Student centers are nice, but often students use the library as a place to be productive and social because learning is a social activity. Many successful school librarians can tell you about how the library becomes a refuge for students who don't fit in or who are seeking a place to bond with other students outside of athletics. Corporate libraries are interesting places that often mix company workers with people from other fields and disciplines that have come to use resources and expertise. Government libraries, such as the Library of Congress, create fellowship programs to encourage scholars from around the world to come and interact with government employees and policy makers.

This concept of the library as community space is hardly new. I've already talked about the ancient Library of Alexandria that was built with colonnades and rooms to maximize the interaction and discussions of scholars. Technology and a renewed focus on the community are allowing us to reclaim libraries for communities. You should expect your library to be a community space—a place for the interchange of ideas and the creation of whole new concepts.

This, however, turns us once again back to your responsibility. A building alone can do nothing. Simply building a structure—no matter how grand, or how representative of the community aesthetic—is not enough. Cramming a beautiful building full of books does not a library make. It takes a community commitment and a group of dedicated facilitators to truly transform brick-and-mortar into knowledge and community. Luckily these facilitators exist, and we call them librarians.

7. Librarians: Expect Brilliance

While you may not have noticed it, throughout this book I have been engaged in a semantic lie. I have talked about what libraries do or don't do, should or shouldn't do. The fact is that libraries can't do anything—they are buildings or rooms. The best you can say is that libraries shield you from the rain and exert gravity. Even the larger concept of a library as an abstract organization is a conceit. The work and impact of libraries is a result of people. These people include paraprofessionals, volunteers, board members, janitors, and guards. However, this work and impact are a direct result of librarians.

There are three basic ways to become a librarian: you are hired as one, you are educated as one, or you grow into being one. The first is the easiest and often least effective way. The second is the norm often mandated by law and probably the most effective way. The last is rare but can be incredibly powerful. Let us take these in turn and talk about the potential positives and pitfalls of each, plus a little of what we can expect from each as well.

Librarian by Hire

In rural Vermont very few people get a graduate degree to be a librarian. The amount of money they would pay in tuition would never be matched by the income they would get, even as the director of a library.

In many rural communities in the Southwest, a good number of library directors work part time. There are plenty of people who work as librarians who have no formal training in the field of librarianship.

This is not restricted to just rural public libraries either. James Billington is the Librarian of Congress—his background is working as a historian. In fact, for centuries the heads of the libraries in colleges and universities were professors and humanities scholars.

There are some advantages to hiring non-professional librarians. They bring in new perspectives. They are cheaper in terms of salaries. They can have more ties to the library's community than someone hired from outside.

However, there are some rather substantial disadvantages to hiring non-professionals as librarians. They often lack specific skills in facilitation. These can be as basic as organizing library resources or as complex as seeing the bigger picture of the libraries' role in the community and in the larger knowledge infrastructure. Many librarians by hire come in with a building-centric and book-centric view of librarianship.

The key to being a successful librarian by hire is a dedication to and support for continuous learning and training. States such as Vermont have active State Libraries that make it part of their mission to prepare librarians. These State Libraries provide workshops, online training, and even site visits to help prepare all librarians to do the job. You should expect your library staff, no matter what their background, to engage in continuous development and training. This means that you should also expect to support travel costs and time off for training.

Or, of course, you can hire a trained librarian…

Librarian by Degree

The standard for preparing librarians is a master's degree in library and information science. In the United States, these programs are accredited by the American Library Association, and as of this writing there are about 60 such programs in North America. (Full disclosure: I work at one of them.) Probably the question students attending a graduate program in library science most often get is "you need a master's degree for that?"

I hope that this is not your question after reading to this point, but I understand why people ask it. After all, much of a librarian's job is to make certain things easier for people and, therefore, they tend to shield communities from the workings of the library. We will delve much deeper into what we should expect from librarians later in this chapter. In the meantime, let me talk about the skills librarians gain from a graduate education.

According to the American Library Association, degreed librarians should be expert in a curriculum that:

"is concerned with recordable information and knowledge, and the services and technologies to facilitate their management and use. The curriculum of library and information studies encompasses information and knowledge creation, communication, identification, selection, acquisition, organization and description, storage and retrieval, preservation, analysis, interpretation, evaluation, synthesis, dissemination, and management."[80]

In their studies librarians are introduced to a wide range of skills useful in libraries and, as it turns out, increasingly useful in other settings like, say, Google and other Fortune 500 companies. Degreed librarians work in libraries, certainly, but they also work as information architects, competitive intelligence officers, even as an executive vice president and head of mortgage servicing at JPMorgan Chase.[81] There are hundreds of librarians employed at publishers and database providers whose products are used throughout academia.

Librarians use their education and skills to identify the needs of a community and build systems to access resources to match the queries (and aspirations) of that community. This can mean creating systems for how items are shelved or how pages are linked on the web. What most people don't realize is that when Tim Berners-Lee invented the World Wide Web, he was trying to solve a library problem—how to find cited physics papers in a digital environment. Librarians are ultimately tool builders.

Does the degree matter? Recall the discussion of school librarians and test scores in Chapter 4. Study after study shows that the presence of a degreed librarian in a school has direct and positive impacts on test scores and retention. That is after controlling for factors like the room, the collection, demographics, and so on. It was the educated and certified librarian, not the library, that made schools better.

Degreed librarians are ready to work, they have a deep knowledge of the field, and they have immediately useful skills. They are experts in not only the day-to-day functioning of a particular library, but have broadly

---

[80] American Library Association, Office for Accreditation. (2008). Standards for accreditation of master's programs in library & information tudies. Retrieved from http://www.ala.org/accreditedprograms/sites/ala.org.accreditedprograms/files/content/standards/standards_2008.pdf

[81] http://www.syr.edu/trustees/inductees/larsen.html (accessed May 7, 2012)

applicable skills and a wide world-view to help communities in trying times.

However, library schools can also imbue these graduates with a book-and-building mentality that may limit their perspectives. One of the biggest concerns with librarians by degree is what I call Daedalus' Maze. Daedulus, as you may recall, is an incredible engineer from Greek mythology who built a maze so complex even he couldn't escape it. Librarians, too, have engineered some incredible tools through their 3,000 year history. They have used tools like classification to build massive collections of materials with millions of items. Some libraries have used these tools to maintain libraries for centuries. The Bodleian Library at Oxford first opened its door in 1602, for example.[82] Yet these schemas and systems have also been used to create a maze of specialties and divisions within the profession. The problem lies in the fact that these tools are based on a specific approach to science and thought called reductionism.

Reductionism is when you take something big and complex and you break it down into smaller and smaller parts until you understand these parts. Then you can add up how all the small parts work and figure out the whole. It is why the Large Hadron Collider exists—take an atom and keep breaking it down until you find its smallest part. So libraries can take the world and break it into smaller and smaller topics allowing someone some precision in finding the parts.

For example, in 1863 Roger Bacon thought the world of ideas could be broken into three parts: memory (stuff about history), reason (stuff about philosophy), and imagination (stuff about the arts). It was a system later adopted by Thomas Jefferson, who used it to organize his considerable collection of books, a collection he later sold to the Congress of the United States to replace the Library of Congress after the British burned the first one. Back in 1732, Samuel Johnson thought he needed only two classes: philology, the study of words and other signs; and philosophy, the study of things signified by them.

However, of all the folks who thought they could classify the world, the one you probably most associate with libraries is Melvil Dewey. Dewey was a librarian and also a passionate advocate for both spelling reform (he would have spelled his name as Dui), and—wait for it—the metric system. This all came together in, as he would tell it, a revelation in church that would later become the Dewey Decimal System (decimal—metric…get it?).

He thought that all the books and materials in the world could be divided into ten categories:

[82] http://www.bodleian.ox.ac.uk/bodley/about/history (accessed May 8, 2012)

- 000 – Computer science, information and general works
- 100 – Philosophy and psychology
- 200 – Religion
- 300 – Social sciences
- 400 – Language
- 500 – Science (including mathematics)
- 600 – Technology and applied science
- 700 – Arts and recreation
- 800 – Literature
- 900 – History and geography

Each of these numbers could be further broken down into more specific topics. So, while books on history are all in the 900's, books on African history would be in the 960's, and the history of Egypt and Sudan would be in 962. Then you start adding numbers after the decimal point to get to an even more specific topic.

The beauty of Dewey's system is that the numbers can stay the same, but you can change the words to accommodate other languages (and changes in national borders). This ability to capture a wide variety of topics and languages, plus some downright excellent salesmanship by Dewey, helped his system to take off internationally. How has reductionism impacted librarians? The same way it has impacted your doctor.

If you break your leg you go to an orthopedist, unless it was a bone in your foot, then you go to a podiatrist. If your heart needs help, off to a cardiologist, unless it needs to be repaired, then you need a cardiothoracic surgeon. You get my point? We don't just have librarians, we have public librarians and academic librarians. We have reference academic librarians, and academic cataloging librarians. Take a look at the American Library Association. It has 11 major divisions (one for academic libraries, one for public, one for catalogers, one for librarians working with youth, etc.). It also has 18 offices to do the work of the organization (one for diversity, one for international relations, etc.). But wait, there's more. It lists 20 Roundtables…kind of like divisions, but not that big (intellectual freedom, library history, games and gaming, and so on). Then there are committees, task forces, and special working groups. It is so complex that at the annual conference you need a web-based program to find events related to your interests.

Why is this a problem? Because, as professionals in medicine are learning, your heart does not work alone. Your heart is part of a complex system. It may be affected by how your lungs work, or disease, or even how often you floss your teeth. This is the problem with reductionism in general; life is more complex than universal systems like the Dewey Decimal System allow for. While a book on faith healing or homeopathic remedies might belong in religion for some communities, it may well be considered medicine for others

This is why librarians, hired or degreed, must become more flexible and holistic. Yes, they need to keep their values and mission in place, but the tools and organizational forms should be fluid. In science, both physical and social, we are seeing that if you take a complex system and break it down into its constituent parts and then put it back together, the whole is greater than the sum of its parts. A community is not simply a lot of people with their individual needs. A community is a set of needs and dreams and skills that, when intermixed, lead to whole new strengths, weaknesses, and dynamics.

Too often, degreed librarians (and the faculty who teach them) get stuck in the reductionist paradigm. Too often, degreed librarians use this reductionist approach to dismiss or ignore innovation and good ideas that come from outside of their specialization. You should expect more.

Librarian by Spirit

The third class of librarians is people who do not have library degrees, and may not have the word "librarian" in their job titles, but who clearly have the same mission, skill set, and service outlook as the profession. People like David Rumsey.

Rumsey made a fortune in real estate and used that money to build an amazing collection of maps. He built himself a room full of maps. Now, that alone does not make Rumsey a librarian in spirit. Lots of folks who have done well build collections. What makes Rumsey noteworthy is that he also used his personal resources to digitize his maps and put them online. He then built a suite of tools to allow anyone to view the maps, compare them, and analyze their own maps. In essence, Rumsey facilitated learning by map lovers, college students, K-12 students, and geographers. This dedication not to simply collecting stuff, but using collections (and software and experts) as tools to facilitate knowledge creation makes him a librarian. This is a point that was recognized by the Institute of Museum and Library Services (IMLS), the federal agency responsible for funding of libraries and museums.

All around your community are these "citizen librarians." In Syracuse and Wisconsin and around the country, individuals and community groups unaffiliated with any library are building Little Free Libraries—mini book boxes. The containers are designed locally and installed at street corners and in people's yards. The community is encouraged both to take and leave books. It is not the books that make these containers into libraries, however; it is the dedication to the community good and learning.

So, we know these are the ways one becomes a librarian. What exactly do librarians do? What should you expect from a librarian?

Salzburg and a Few of My Favorite Things

To answer the question of what to expect from a librarian I need to take you to Salzburg, Austria. Over the mountain from the picturesque city is a schloss (a castle). It is a castle you probably know, because it was the inspiration and partial set for the von Trapp family manor in the movie *The Sound of Music*. The building is called Schloss Leopoldskron, and it is now the home of the Salzburg Global Seminar. The Seminar was started by three Harvard students right after World War II and was intended to be a sort of training ground for emerging leaders of a new Europe. Today, the Seminar has broadened to a global scope and brings together leaders from around the world on topics as varied as global governance, culture, education, and finance.

On October 19, 2011, a group of library and museum innovators from over 31 countries gathered in Salzburg to discuss "Libraries and Museums in an Era of Participatory Culture."[83] I was lucky enough to be invited. Through plenary panels and intensive break-out groups, the seminar fellows developed a series of recommendations and strategies for libraries and museums in the era of Facebook.

One of those groups was charged with developing recommendations around skills needed by librarians and museum professionals in today's connected and participatory world. Rather than focusing solely on new skills or separate skills for librarians and museum professionals, the group developed a framework for a comprehensive and joint library/museum curriculum. In essence, the group focused on what librarians and museum professionals need to know, realizing that participatory culture has ramifications for new skills and traditional functions alike.

Much of this curriculum would not surprise you even before you read this book.

Librarians (my focus here) need to know technology. Specifically you should expect your librarians:

- To engage and evolve with technology.
- To impart technology to the community across generations.
- To create and maintain an effective virtual presence.

[83] Mack, D. L. (2011, October 19–23). Libraries and museums in an era of participatory culture. Session 482 Report, Salzburg Global Seminar in partnership with Institute of Museum and Library Services. Retrieved
from http://www.imls.gov/assets/1/AssetManager/SGS_Report_2012.pdf

- To use technology to crowdsource and reach out to the community in a collaborative way (in other words, not a brochure-ware like static website, but one the community can use and help build).

Librarians should be skilled in asset management. This includes all the inventory skills we talked about, like cataloging, as well as preserving memories and materials for future generations and building collections when necessary. However, this is not limited to books and shelves (or in the case of museums, mummies in cases). This also includes safeguarding assets that are meant for regular use.

I have mentioned ideas like the prejudice library where libraries circulate more than just books and DVDs. There are public libraries that circulate fishing poles near rivers and libraries that circulate puppets. At the Fab Lab in Fayetteville they will be circulating cameras and book-making materials. In Brooklyn they have an on-demand printing press that will print out bound books written by the community. In Africa they are circulating ceremonial masks; at Onondaga Community College you can check out models of body parts and vivisected cats for anatomy classes. My point here is that you should expect librarians to build living collections that the community needs and guarantee the availability of these resources for the whole community.

The next set of skills specified in the Salzburg Curriculum revolves around culture. You should expect librarians to be good communicators, not the stereotypically shy, mousy wallflowers. Librarians should be able to actively reach out to all sectors of a community, to understand the social mores of those community parts, and to bridge these different classes and strata.

Now, it would be easy to read that and think it just applies to public libraries. However, as a member of academia I can tell you there are plenty of cultural divides in higher education. Talking to faculty, then students, then administration can be like using three different languages. Likewise, school librarians have to understand not only the differences between teachers and students, but math teachers, and music teachers, and English teachers.

For too long too many librarians have holed up in their libraries and tried to create their own culture for the community to adjust to. It may be cloaked in terms like "creating a haven for readers" or "enhancing the atmosphere for scholars," but make no mistake, these librarians are creating boundaries, not bridging them.

Let me be clear: the work of the librarian is specialized and it is hard. Navigating the conflicted and sprawling knowledge infrastructure for the right article or expert or resources takes professional preparation and a dedication found in other high-level information professions. And like those other professions, librarianship has developed a specialized language. For every bit of technobabble to come out of Silicon Valley, a librarian can find a corresponding bit of seemingly incoherent library-terminology. For every Retina Display LTE tablet there is a MARC record referencing an authority file to create a holdings record.

Being able to unlock walled gardens and a myriad of sources and then weave information into a comprehensive and comprehendible whole is one of the most valuable skills in a knowledge economy. That said, part of that work is to make the result easy to understand and use, not to make the community members into little librarians. You should expect your librarian to speak your language, and the librarian should expect you to respect that doing so is valuable work.

The Salzburg curriculum specifies a set of skills around knowledge and learning. You should expect your librarian to be an effective trainer and understand how you seek information, how you synthesize new knowledge, and finally how to help you spread that new knowledge among the community.

You should expect your librarian to be a professional able to manage a library operation. This includes understanding funding, making projects and services sustainable, and doing all this in an ethical manner. A librarian, as a professional, needs to be able to assess the impact of library services and communicate that impact to the community. No more assuming a library is a universal good. How did the library help fulfill the needs and the aspirations of the community—specifically?

These competencies are not radical departures from how we have prepared librarians for decades—at least on the surface. There is one set of skills introduced in the Salzburg curriculum that is new: librarians must be skilled in Transformative Social Engagement.

A community should be a better place because it contains a library. Better means change—from how it is to something better. The library and librarians should add value to the community. If you add something like value, you change something. So bottom line, a librarian should help guide a community through a continuous change process. Feel free to revisit the whole jackbooted librarians discussion in the "Improve Society" chapter—we know that this change is not solely a matter of the librarian enacting a vision of change. It is also the librarian working with the community, facilitating the change.

How do librarians actively, and in some cases, proactively, engage in change? They must be able to identify community needs. They must be able to help the community organize around those needs, including understanding those needs in light of larger community agendas (like economic development, for example). They must be able to facilitate activism by the community. Librarians must be practiced in the art of negotiation and conflict management. They must help the community understand how these initiatives can be sustained over time.

For too long librarians have seen service as standing ready to serve. You must expect them to understand that no one changed the world by standing ready.

The Facilitators

So librarians have skills around technology, asset management, cultural skills, and transformative social engagement. They use these skills toward their mission: to improve society through facilitating knowledge creation in their communities. Yet there's a funny thing about that mission statement. I developed that statement for a part of a book written for librarians called the *Atlas of New Librarianship*. But I have had publishers say "that's my mission." And I have journalists say, "that's my mission." I've also heard it from educators and even civil servants. And here's the thing, they are all right.

More and more, information professions are wrestling with an ever more connected society where information is readily available. More professions are coming to understand the importance of social interactions and the complexities of community. Because of that, many professions have found themselves in increasingly close and sometimes disconcerting proximity to other professions.

Some librarians see this newfound proximity as a threat. These librarians retreat to what they have done historically, seeking a sort of safe boundary. There is a real problem with defining your profession by functions and tools rather than impact and mission. Once you begin to define yourself by what is it you do, new ways of doing things become threats. Or worse, anyone who does similar things becomes competition. Google is a threat because it doesn't use descriptive cataloging to index the world. So some librarians seek to dismiss it. Amazon is competition because it provides books. Worse yet, it is even letting folks borrow books on Kindles.

And what is the response to these so-called threats? Did librarians build a new Google, or their own eBook platform? No, instead they have adopted Google and Amazon because it turns out these tools work. Never mind that Google is the largest advertising agency in the world, and Amazon is now able to mine your reading history. If librarians and the communities that support them define the world through functional eyes of threats and competition, librarians do not engage new players as partners, nor do they effectively work to instill their values within their services. Too many librarians see what works, and use that tool nearly ignorant of the cost to themselves and those they serve.

Please do not misunderstand me: I use Google and Amazon. I use Facebook and Twitter. There is great value in these tools for librarians and for the community. However, all of these services can be made better through partnering with libraries. Where librarians can learn about new ways of discovering information or packaging content, these new partners can learn from a 3,000-year history of community engagement and a well-defined value system. However, this will only happen if librarians are open to true partnership and seen as valuable allies. If librarians are seen instead as isolated and stuck with functions of the past, why partner?

This is also true of professions like teaching and journalism. In some communities, local papers and public libraries are creating a sort of merger. Journalists are learning from librarians about inviting the community in as part of the news beat.

More teachers are adopting inquiry-based methods of learning. Many publishers are starting to give up the concept of gatekeeper to quality, and instead looking to spark conversations in readers. While it is beyond the scope of this book, a science of facilitation is emerging. It has the potential to radically change the knowledge professions and the knowledge infrastructure of your community. You should expect your librarians to lead the way and look to create knowledge teams of diverse players to meet the needs of your community.

The potential power of a group of allied facilitating professions can be summed up in a concept like "Publisher of Community" and can be seen in the rural hills of Vermont. I have mentioned before that Vermont wired the state and provided high bandwidth Internet connections to libraries in rural areas. There is more to this story.

The State Library had to convince the rural libraries to pay for this access. The cost was not a lot of money, about $100 per month for an amazing amount of bandwidth. Still, it was more than the nothing libraries were paying for, which was, in essence, a dialup connection. At the roll out meeting for the project, one of the project partners was getting a bit frustrated with perceived resistance, so she took to the stage and said (I'm paraphrasing here), "I don't think you are getting this. We are offering you a service that should cost hundreds of thousands of dollars. Think of your connection now like a dirt path. This would be like bringing the autobahn to your front door." I could almost see the eyes of the librarians in the room getting larger—in terror. I could see visions of hundreds of German headlights racing towards them at 100 miles an hour.

These libraries were looking at this Internet connection as a new type of book. The rural communities they served would come in and be able to consume things faster. That was not the point of the project, however.

The fast connection was coming to the libraries, but it wasn't meant to stop there, and it wasn't meant for just really fast (and I'm talking *really* fast) web browsing. The connection was meant to spread to local businesses, hospitals, newspapers, and eventually homes. And it was meant not to just bring the world to rural Vermont but to unleash rural Vermont on the world.

Libraries could team up with local papers to publish news and events to neighboring communities. Local schools could use real time, high definition video conferencing to share classes. So if one small school couldn't afford a French teacher, it could put together a class of students from eight schools. Local businesses could now trade their wares globally. Local artists could collaborate across the state. People leaving city life could relocate to rural counties and keep their jobs telecommuting. In essence, the connection was like a new type of printing press, and what was being printed was the community itself.

This is exactly the mission of libraries. Teaming with allied missions in journalism and publishing and teaching and health care expands the impact of libraries and the other fields. The librarian can weave together a connective fabric that encompasses the whole community in a way that no one else can. Likewise, academic libraries can weave together departments and publish the work of a college or university and disseminate it to the world. School libraries can broadcast student projects and teachers' lesson plans out to the community and invite participation in the educational process by parents, government, and business alike.

You should expect your librarians to help form this publisher of the community; not in isolation, but with a rich and diverse set of actors.

Adding Up a Librarian

So what is a librarian if not a degree, if not a mission statement in isolation, and if not a set of functions? I would argue that a librarian is the intersection of three things: the mission, the means of facilitation, and the values librarians bring to a community. We've already covered the first two (approach to mission and facilitation), but what about values?

Librarians hold these professional values: service, learning, openness, intellectual freedom and safety, and intellectual honesty. That is, librarians seek to serve, so the value of their work is measurable only in the impact it has on others. They value learning, so their impact is measured by how well others gain knowledge. They value openness, so the means that librarians use to facilitate learning are observable and transparent. Librarians value intellectual freedom and safety because the best learning happens in the richest knowledge environment possible. And librarians value intellectual honesty so the learner is guaranteed an honest guide through the learning process.

I have already touched on some of these. However, there is one value I need to expand upon for a moment: intellectual honesty. Some of you will note that I did not include "unbiased" in that list of values. That is because we cannot be unbiased. As humans, we instill our values, prejudices, and our own worldview into all that we do. The language you use, the color of your skin, the place you grew up, your education all influence how you see and interact with the world. You are not unbiased. Librarians believe that privacy is essential—that is a bias. Librarians believe that more views of a topic are better than fewer—that is a bias. Librarians believe, I hope, that librarians and libraries serve a vital role in a democracy—that too is a bias. We cannot be unbiased, but we can be intellectually honest.

Take the sciences. I am an information scientist. Scientists have not only acknowledged that we have biases but have even come up with measures to quantify them. Yet people still look at science as a legitimate way of examining the world. Why? Not because scientists as people are objective and neutral but because scientists have developed unbiased tools and an ethos of intellectual honesty. As a scientist I acknowledge my methods may be flawed, so I report them for examination. I acknowledge my interpretation of the data may be wrong, so I publish my results. Science knows the difference between unbiased and transparent. You should expect librarians to adopt this distinction also.

8. Action Plan: Expect More

There is a saying that you shouldn't muster the troops without giving them marching orders. In other words, it is fine for me to tell you what to expect, but without an action plan to get you there it is only an exercise. You may recall that earlier in the book I said that bad libraries build collections, good libraries build services, and great libraries build communities. This makes a pretty good outline for an action plan: what to do if you have a bad, good or great library.

Action Plan for Great Libraries

Some of you already have libraries and librarians that exceed your expectations. Wonderful. Your action plan is simple: support them. This is not just about money but also about letting them hear your voice and share your dreams, and taking ownership in the library itself. You need to spread the word that your library is alive and well and is more than what folks expect.

There are plenty of people out there who think the era of libraries has passed. I talked to one board member who loves his library, but said that every time he mentioned to someone that he was on the board he got a sympathetic "Aw, that's too bad." It happens to me all the time. (It's one of the reasons I wrote this book.) When people ask me what I do, "I'm a professor of library science," I say. "Oh," they say, "I love books, too," or sometimes with less tact, "We still need libraries?" If we love our libraries and they support our needs, we should support them right back.

I believe that many of these less-than-supportive views of libraries come from interactions with libraries in the past that have set the bar too low. Eli Neiburger once said that for teens, the library is a net detractor of social capital. He would see teens at the library looking down at the floor and telling their parents they hoped they wouldn't be seen. The library wasn't cool, wasn't fun, wasn't helpful. However, Eli and the Ann Arbor District Library changed that. Eli started a gaming tournament at the library. It was co-organized by teens themselves. Once a month teens from around the area would compete for top rankings in games like *Mario Kart* for the Wii.

Eli went further than just having a room and a Wii. He would stream an ESPN-like show about the tournament out on public access TV and the web. Then at the end of the tournament he would post the result on the web. Suddenly he found teen boys flocking not only to the library for the tournament but to the website to show their friends how good they were. Gaming transformed the library from a net detractor to a net adder of social capital. He raised teens' expectations of the library, and the community rallied around to support it.

Why gaming in the library, by the way? Because, as a great librarian will tell you, gaming is central to the lives and learning of teens—and just about everyone else. Kids learn to read through games. Teens learn to solve problems through games. College students study to get jobs in the gaming industry. Adults use games to stay mentally active. Communities across the country have adopted gaming as a way to socialize (*Words with Friends*, anyone?), relax, and learn. Great libraries understand this; bad libraries think it's "Pizza, pizza, pizza, book!"

That line comes from a hilarious video that a group of librarians put together about getting college students into the library[84]. They created the video to make clear that learning isn't restricted to books. Having food in the library, or gaming, or knitting clubs, or people fabricating new parts on a MakerBot is not a method to lure in the public and then hit them up to check out books. These activities are ways of facilitating learning, not loss leader marketing to trick people into a visit to the library.

You should expect a great library to seek out innovative ways of supporting learning. A great library should provoke and prompt conversation. The librarians should expect you to engage in those conversations. They should expect you to question why something is part of a library, and you should expect them to come up with something more than "marketing" or "keeping up with what other libraries are doing."

---

[84] http://youtu.be/ibi7aTmVA_c (accessed June 7, 2012)

To be sure, great libraries require funding. You can't expect a great library to stay that way by cutting staff and replacing true librarians with clerks. However, you should expect a great library to earn and justify that cost. In the midst of the Great Depression, for example, the budget of the New York Public Library actually increased. Why? Because the city saw great value in how the library reached out to a community in need and offered services like education, job retraining, and a suite of social services.

Action Plan for Bad Libraries

Let me be very clear. What makes a library bad is not its collections. Bad libraries can have huge collections or small ones. Great libraries can also have large or small (or no) collections. However, bad libraries see the collection as the materials they buy and lease. Great libraries see the community itself as the collection. There is fantastic value in loads of books and reams of journal articles, but how much more rich and varied and powerful is the community itself?

The true collection is in grandparents, teachers, and students. In the public sphere the community-collection consists of children whose imaginations are unencumbered by the day-to-day realities of the workplace. It is also seniors. The past century has seen the expected lifespan of an American go from 47 to 77. Imagine that vast sea of experience and unbridled talent seeking not profit but a legacy.

In schools, the true collection does not sit on shelves but in the classroom: the honest effort of the learner, the wisdom and patience of teachers. A school community—from nurses and art teachers to athletes and coaches to administrators and parents—is a rich collection indeed.

In universities, where the focus is on discovering new knowledge and preparing the next workforce, the collection spans the institution. There, the scholar is unlocking the mysteries of the universe and the lecturer is making those secrets accessible to students. The collection extends to alumni and funders and groundskeepers, all struggling to push society's knowledge to new heights.

What collection of books or magazines in a corporate setting could rival the knowledge of engineers or lawyers or doctors?

The community is the true collection, and bad libraries need to spend a lot less time on collections of books and a lot more time on connections within the community. A bad library talks about building collections for the next generation; a great library understands that the value it delivers is a community's appreciation of heritage and aspirations for a legacy. Bad libraries seek to build connections between items, and great libraries build links between people.

It is not the shape or state of the building (or room) that constitutes a bad library. There is a fantastic library at the heart of the U.S. Embassy in Rome that is little more than a set of desks, yet effectively serves diplomats all around Italy and the world. I have been in fabulous library buildings where the very architecture oozes intellect and a temple-like reverence—yet they are nearly empty because the community doesn't even know they exist.

A bad library will use the building as an excuse. The case will be made that the public/students/professionals will flock to the library with better parking or a bigger set of book stacks. And that is true. For weeks after new building opens it will be filled with the curious. However, it is ultimately the services, professionals, and co-ownership that will bring people back. You build a new library when the old one is too small to accommodate the community, not when it is too small to accommodate the stuff.

I was on a public library board. The central library had been moved from an older Carnegie building to a new downtown shopping mall some years ago. It was part of the county's attempt to get community members to come back to downtown. By the time I joined the board a decade or so later, the mall was in pretty bad shape and the number of visits to the library was declining. The director at the time, who had come in well after the move, kept talking about a lack of parking, even though the parking garage below the mall had more space than the old Carnegie building had. The director said the decline in use was because there was no off-street access to the library—folks had to go into the mall and up an elevator to find the library.

The deputy county executive who had been instrumental in moving the library had heard enough. The next board meeting, he brought in poster-sized charts showing an increase in library use after the move. He then showed how the decrease in library services and budget during a recession had been the reason for the initial decline in use. He made it clear that there had been no subsequent recovery of visits once the economy had improved after the new library director had arrived. It was a rather startling reminder that expecting more of a library includes expecting better use of data and getting past excuses.

This is all fine and good, but how do you turn things around? First, realize that people love libraries, even bad ones. For some community members the thought that there are "bad" libraries is a sort of assault. All around, libraries are being loved to death. People believe in libraries but don't use them. Or they use them but don't challenge them to be better, or to even justify their work. One large urban public library I worked with ran over 20,000 programs a year. These included story hours for kids, and lecture series with world famous authors. Why 20,000? Would 10,000 have had the same impact? How many people benefited from these programs? How do they know? What held these programs together as a sort of theme or tied them to the library's mission?

As a community member you must, in the words of Saint Paul, "test everything; retain what is good."[85] To question something is not to assume something is bad, but to test its fitness. We would be horrified if we went to the doctor and she used leeches to bleed us when we had the flu. Tools change, methods change, and yet the profession, mission, and values endure. Asking why a library offers reference services, or why its collection budget needs to be increased, or about the impact of a story hour is not out of bounds. Great libraries welcome the questions because they are a chance to show value.

So here is your game plan for turning around a bad library.

Educate yourself

This book is short; it was written for busy people. I've tried to point to more information on the examples and ideas presented here. Follow up. Look for great libraries, not to copy, but to get inspired. There are great libraries and librarians out there, and the great thing about them is that—as a by-product of maintaining constant and sustained conversation with their communities—a lot of their work is easily visible and well documented.

Play

As I have said, every community is unique, and a great library does not simply take a service from another library and put it in place without considering local conditions. Also realize that great libraries play. Staff are given time to experiment and try out new ideas. Some libraries have surfing days when staff get together, surf the web, and shout out great new tools and links for others to try. You should expect librarians to try out the latest web service, if only to peek at it. Good libraries do this too, but great libraries invite the public to join in.

The DOK library in Delft, Netherlands, is world famous for being one of, if not the most, innovative library in the world. Its librarians regularly use the space to host art exhibitions and interactive technology petting zoos. Other libraries are partnering with electronics retailers like Best Buy to bring in the latest and greatest toys for the librarians and community members to try.

The Syracuse University Library put on a series of teaching tools events where, for a day, faculty, students, and librarians came to look at new methods of teaching and new educational tools. It wasn't a series of

[85] 1 Thessalonians 5:16-24

hour-long lectures and demos. Instead faculty and staff formed small groups where they tried the techniques and shared notes. Great librarians are not afraid to show they are learning, too; they are not afraid to learn from others, even if they are learning from a nine-year-old. And here is an essential point: *great libraries come from great librarians*.

Great librarians experiment with new services and are not afraid to fail rapidly. There is a difference between a failure and a mistake. A mistake is when you do something wrong and don't learn from it (so you often repeat it). A failure is something you try that is a little bit beyond your reach, but you can figure out how to do it better next time. If your librarians are not trying new things and pushing the boundaries, or are afraid to try something because they might fail—they are afraid of learning (or worse, victims of bad management that rewards only success and not learning).

If every new thing a library does, no matter how big (starting a gaming program) or small (accepting canned foods in place of fines), happens only after the formation of a committee and a three-month planning process, then you are killing innovation and your library is not about learning and playing.

Benchmark

All that said, there is a time when play must end and experiments must transform from experiments to reliable services. This requires knowing what impact or outcomes you want the service to have. These outcomes are agreements between the library and the community. Does a service need a certain number of uses to justify it? Is it more important to build the library's reputation externally for this service? Good hard play leads to realistic and authentic benchmarks. These benchmarks need to make sense to the community and need to be available for review by the community as well.

Trust your expertise (but be open)

You shouldn't have to become a librarian to understand the value a library provides. Expect your librarians to bridge the gap between their world and yours. There is an old line I use that goes, "The techies never say no—instead they throw technobabble at you until you go away." ("Well, I would load that software on your machine, but then I'd have to make an exception to the firewall to allow for the https connection or tunnel through the VPN to check the code signature…") Librarians can match the IT folk, acronym for acronym. ("Well I could fix the spelling of your last name on the MARC record, but then I'd have to propagate it through our whole cataloging module of the ILS, and send it up to OCLC to match against the authority list maintained by LC…)

I have seen change-resistant librarians completely stop a very smart board member with this technique. The member wanted to know why cookbooks were in the same place as the books on business. It wasn't just odd, it was downright annoying to be in the middle of a consultation with a librarian on business plans and tax codes only to be interrupted by someone looking for a lemon pie recipe. The answer she got was, "They are together in the Dewey Decimal System," which is true. Why? Because Dewey saw home economics and cookery (his term for cooking) as the female equivalent of business...did I mention Dewey was a misogynist?

So case closed, right? Well, not really. Even though the Dewey numbers go together, there is nothing that says the books have to. You can put the cookbooks wherever you damn well please, so long as folks can find them. Even Dewey would have said that.

You are the expert on your needs and you have expertise in your community. Trust that. If something doesn't seem to make sense, ask. If you get an answer that doesn't make sense, ask again (and again). Libraries are there to make you smarter, so when they make you feel dumb, something is wrong.

Now just as the value of play has to be matched with the rigor of benchmarks, so, too, does your personal view need to be open to the views of others. As I've said, communities are rich and multifaceted places. Often times there are conflicts between what one group wants and another group needs. A good library helps mediate this difference and find common ground. Take the Freegal service I mentioned before (downloading MP3 files for personal use at taxpayer expense). I know a lot of great libraries that offer the service. They offer it even though they don't believe it is the best value for the community. They offer the service because the community made an informed decision and feels that, while the benefit may be limited to the community as whole, the value that the smaller population receives translates into more resources and support for other library services.

Visit

I have yet to find a great librarian who doesn't like to show off a little bit. They are born teachers, and their service ethic means that if they can share something to help you, they will. Take the time to travel and see other libraries. Get ideas, see what works, talk to the librarians and the community in the library. But make sure you talk to the librarians. What you want to get out of the visit is not just a sense of the architecture and how busy a library is, but the decisions and process that lead to that situation.

For example, there is something called virtual reference in libraries. Through the web, you can ask librarians questions, and those librarians, either in real time or through email, will help you find the answer. Several years ago it was a new thing in libraries and so there were conferences and there was some peer pressure to start up a service.

At one of these conferences I talked with a librarian and asked her what her library did about virtual reference. Somewhat sheepishly, she said that her library didn't do virtual reference. I asked her to describe her library to me. "It is a small all-women's college in the Northeast. It is the kind of place where at 9 o'clock at night the students walk the 20 feet from their dorms to the library in their PJs to study."

I said to her, "Don't ever offer virtual reference." At the time the common wisdom was to offer virtual reference, but here the librarian saw past the peer pressure to the community need.

I know it may be asking a lot of you to study up on libraries. Well, if you have made it this far in the book, you probably are already inclined to do so, but still, why bother going out and seeing other libraries? Because part of being human is that we are very bad at describing what we want without referencing something we already know. It is how we build knowledge; we scaffold new discoveries upon the top of what we already know. The richer that foundation, the richer the knowledge.

This was brought home to me quite eloquently by Cindy Granell, an elementary school librarian, when she talked about what her board of education knew about elementary school libraries. This is what she told me. The average age of school board members in the States is between 40 and 59.[86] Take those 40-year-old school board members. Do a little math, and you realize the last time they used an elementary school library was right around 1980…before the web and before most people had personal computers (and when the average cost of a PC was approaching $4,000). Back then, school libraries were places where books were the core tool librarians had to work with. Today, school library curriculum includes cyberbullying, finding credible information, how to search in databases, and research skills, among other things. In an iPad age when every new TV comes with a Facebook app, these librarians have 18 hours a year (30 minutes once a week) to help kids become both good readers and effective participants in the knowledge infrastructure. If these board members never step foot in the library, how would they know that?

This is not just a school issue either. Study after study shows that the primary influence for new scholars' use of information technology and information resources is their mentor or primary advisor. That means that most scholars are at least one generation removed from current practice. Without actively going out and seeing what is available today, how do today's new scholars know how much better it could be?

---

[86] In Middle Township, 'age is no barrier to leadership.' (2007, January 18). *New Jersey's School Board Recognition, 30*(21). Retrieved from *http://www.njsba.org/sb_notes/20070118/recog.html*

Create Forums

One of the funniest (in a sad sort of way) things I have seen in a library came when students protested the off-site storage plan Syracuse University had proposed. Graduate students congregated in the first floor of the library ready to hand out angry missives about the library...except they didn't bring enough copies. So the librarians helped them make the copies. The students sought signatures for a petition. The librarians suggested they could do the petition online as well and showed the students how. When the protestors got hungry, the librarians directed them to the café in the library.

Now this wasn't actually the librarians joining in the protest; they disagreed pretty fundamentally. But the librarians knew their mission was not to shut down the conversation, but to facilitate it...so they did. To be sure, they also pitched their case to the protestors (like the commons space they were against was the same space they were now using to protest). But they welcomed the conversation and were professionals who did their jobs.

How do you interact with your library? Does the library have a comment card box? What happens with the cards? Who sees them? Just the librarians? Does the library hold focus groups? Do they have open board meetings that you actually know about before the fact? Does the library have a series of advisory boards? It always amazes me that public librarians wonder why more teens never come to the library when the library never felt it important to put a teen on the board, or at least on a board for teen services. Does your library have a brownbag series where librarians and the community can gather to listen to speakers (in person or online) and then talk about it? How many times have you sat down with a librarian in your office?

Ask to see your library's "conversation plan." They will probably say they don't know what that is because I just made up the phrase. But it will be a great departure point for talking about how the library formally, regularly, and in an assessable way talks to the community. This is *not* a marketing plan that speaks to letting the community know what the library is up to. You should expect librarians to have a list of outreach partners (academic departments, the Chamber of Commerce, etc.). There should be a sense of a schedule for checking in with these partners.

A great example of this sort of planned communications was an academic library director who visited each college in the university every year at budget development time. He brought with him his budget targets and a list of journals and databases the library purchased each year with the associated cost. He then went through the list with the department's faculty, asking what he should keep and what he should cut. The colleges felt as if they were part of the process and saw direct value from the library.

Compare this to another college I worked with as a consultant. The library formed an advisory group of faculty from the different colleges. The sociologist of the group started talking about how it was unfair that the library was spending so much money on the physical sciences, and not enough on the social sciences. The physicist in the group quickly chimed in that he was surprised to hear that, as he always thought the library was ignoring the physical sciences for the social sciences. This library, by not including the community in decision-making, had not only pitted everyone against each other, but had managed to make all of them feel slighted! Co-ownership demands both transparency of decision-making, and power in those decisions. All of this rests upon having an ongoing and facilitated forum for conversational exchange and goal setting for the library.

Map the Conversation

The most effective way of seeing the relationship to the community is not through a list of services or a list of collections. It is not seen in a string of statistics or in strategic plans. It is in the conversations the library chooses to engage in and support.

You should expect your library to work with the community to identify a list of key stakeholders or sub-communities that the library can or should help. In a college, this might be faculty, students, administration, and staff. In a school, it might be teachers, students, and administration. It can be more specific. For example, in my work with a law firm we identified lawyers as a major group, but it was helpful to further break this group down into criminal and civil divisions, and even further into environmental lawyers, civil rights, tax, and so on. The level of resolution can change as the engagement with these groups increases.

Once you have identified these key stakeholders, you need to identify the conversations/problems/aspirations within the groups. So faculty are talking about curriculum development, the Latino population is talking about economic development, etc. Next, map any regularity to these conversations. For example, administrators in a school district have a predictable timetable to develop a budget with state-mandated forums and milestones. Working with a representative group from the community and the library, prioritize these conversations. Which ones can the library help with the most? Which ones should the library be a part of?

Lastly, lay out the services offered by the library and librarians. Try and connect the services to the conversations. Are there services with connections? Are there parts of important conversations with no services? Why? This is a way of embedding library service in the community, not simply identifying what the library does well (or at least does already) and making the most of it. Remember, the mission of the library is to improve society, not maximize the use of services it already offers. Libraries facilitate knowledge creation; they don't wring the value out of collections.[87]

Action Plan for Good Libraries

And what about those libraries that fall in the middle? The difference between a good library and a great library can be subtle. There are some very good libraries out there. These libraries are dedicated to making you happy and serving your needs. They have the latest in materials (books, DVDs, journal articles, etc.). Their websites are well organized and functional. They prize customer service and they get you what you need. They tend to collect a lot of data on the community and have active marketing. Many communities feel these libraries are meeting their expectations.

But if you want to see the difference between a good library and a great one, try visiting a Borders bookstore or a Blockbuster video store. You can't. They don't exist anymore. And when they closed, the only signs you saw were advertising clearance sales and deep discounts. But you know what signs you see when they try and close a great library? Signs of protest. You see picket lines. You see angry town hall meetings. Why? Well, that takes us back to the very first chapter. The reason why is because the library is part of the community. It is not a set of comfy chairs and an excellent collection. It is a symbol, and a friend, and a teacher.

But let's be honest. Some libraries close with nary a whisper. Academic library budgets are downsized and corporations close their libraries. They close bad libraries, yes, but they also close good libraries. The difference between good and great comes down to this: a library that seeks to serve your community is good, and a library that seeks to inspire your community to be better every day is great. You can love a good library, but you need a great library.

When you limit your expectations of a library to a supplier for your consumption, the library is in direct competition with Amazon, Google, and the local paper. But if you expect more—if you expect your library to be an advocate for you in the complex knowledge infrastructure—if you expect your library to be a center of learning and innovation—if you expect your library to help you create knowledge and not simply get you easy access to the work of others—if you expect your librarians to be personally concerned with your success—if you expect the library to be a

---

[87] The process of mapping community conversations is covered in greater depth in the *Atlas of New Librarianship*.

third place that glues together a community—if you expect your library to inspire you, to challenge you, to provoke you, but always to respect you beyond your means to pay—then you expect a great library. You deserve a great library. Go out and get it!

About the Author

R. David Lankes is a professor and Dean's Scholar for the New Librarianship at Syracuse University's School of Information Studies, and director of the Information Institute of Syracuse. Lankes has always been interested in combining theory and practice to create active research projects that make a difference. Past projects include the ERIC Clearinghouse on Information and Technology, the Gateway to Education Materials, AskERIC and the Virtual Reference Desk. Lankes' more recent work involves how participatory concepts can reshape libraries and credibility.

Lankes is a passionate advocate for libraries and their essential role in today's society. He has served on advisory boards and study teams in the fields of libraries, telecommunications, education, and transportation including at the National Academies. He has been a visiting fellow at the National Library of Canada, the Harvard School of Education, and was the first fellow of ALA's Office for Information Technology Policy. His book *The Atlas of New Librarianship* won the 2012 ABC-CLIO/Greenwood Award for the Best Book in Library Literature.

Index—Expect More

WITHDRAWN

Made in the USA
Lexington, KY
19 March 2013